Resources Required to Meet the U.S. Army Reserve's Enlisted Recruiting Requirements Under Alternative Recruiting Goals, Conditions, and Eligibility Policies

BRUCE R. ORVIS, CRAIG A. BOND, DANIEL SCHWAM, IRINEO CABREROS

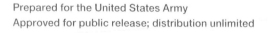

Prepared for the United States Army
Approved for public release; distribution unlimited

 ARROYO CENTER

For more information on this publication, visit **www.rand.org/t/RRA1304-1**.

About RAND

The RAND Corporation is a research organization that develops solutions to public policy challenges to help make communities throughout the world safer and more secure, healthier and more prosperous. RAND is nonprofit, nonpartisan, and committed to the public interest. To learn more about RAND, visit www.rand.org.

Research Integrity

Our mission to help improve policy and decisionmaking through research and analysis is enabled through our core values of quality and objectivity and our unwavering commitment to the highest level of integrity and ethical behavior. To help ensure our research and analysis are rigorous, objective, and nonpartisan, we subject our research publications to a robust and exacting quality-assurance process; avoid both the appearance and reality of financial and other conflicts of interest through staff training, project screening, and a policy of mandatory disclosure; and pursue transparency in our research engagements through our commitment to the open publication of our research findings and recommendations, disclosure of the source of funding of published research, and policies to ensure intellectual independence. For more information, visit www.rand.org/about/research-integrity.

RAND's publications do not necessarily reflect the opinions of its research clients and sponsors.

Published by the RAND Corporation, Santa Monica, Calif.
© 2022 RAND Corporation
RAND® is a registered trademark.

Library of Congress Cataloging-in-Publication Data is available for this publication.
ISBN: 978-1-9774-0956-0

About This Report

This report documents research and analysis conducted as part of a project entitled *Recruiting Resource Model for Army Reserve Enlistment Mission*, sponsored by the Assistant Secretary of the Army for Manpower and Reserve Affairs. The purpose of the project was to develop a model that determines the expected resource costs necessary to achieve the U.S. Army Recruiting Command (USAREC), Regular Army (RA), and U.S. Army Reserve (USAR) mission, including recruiters, incentives, and marketing dollars and, based on the integrated RA-USAR model, develop an optimization algorithm and tool that determines the efficient allocation of resources to achieve RA and USAR recruiting objectives.

This research was conducted within RAND Arroyo Center's Personnel, Training, and Health Program. RAND Arroyo Center, part of the RAND Corporation, is a federally funded research and development center (FFRDC) sponsored by the United States Army.

RAND operates under a "Federal-Wide Assurance" (FWA00003425) and complies with the *Code of Federal Regulations for the Protection of Human Subjects Under United States Law* (45 CFR 46), also known as "the Common Rule," as well as with the implementation guidance set forth in Department of Defense (DoD) Instruction 3216.02. As applicable, this compliance includes reviews and approvals by RAND's Institutional Review Board (Human Subjects Protection Committee) and by the U.S. Army. The views of sources utilized in this study are solely their own and do not represent the official policy or position of DoD or the U.S. government.

Contents

Figures and Tables

Figures

Tables

Summary

This report presents research intended to enhance the effectiveness and efficiency of recruiting resource allocation and enlistment eligibility policies. The Reserve Recruiting Resource Model (RRRM) optimizes the recruiting resource levels and mix needed to achieve future U.S. Army Reserve (USAR) recruiting goals under changing enlisted accession requirements and recruiting environments (as characterized by present and expected future economic conditions) and alternative eligibility policies for potential recruits, as well as allowing comparison of alternative courses of action.[1]

As discussed in the report on the Recruiting Resource Model for the active component (Knapp et al., 2018), the U.S. Army spent on average $1.6 billion annually in 2020 dollars on recruiting resources (including recruiter compensation) from fiscal year (FY) 2001 to FY 2014, and nearly $2.0 billion annually in FY 2008 and FY 2009.[2] Cost reflects both the recruiting environment and the accession mission.

The Army has several levers at its disposal to try and meet its recruiting mission, with resources jointly used for both Regular Army (RA) and USAR accessions. These recruiting resources, such as recruiters, enlistment bonuses, and advertising, differ in their cost per additional recruit produced and the lead time necessary to change individual resourcing levels (with enlistment bonuses generally the fastest and changes in recruiter numbers generally the slowest). The Army can also modify recruit eligibility policies to help it achieve its accession requirement within available resources. It has, at times, granted more enlistment waivers, taken more soldiers with prior military service, and recruited more persons without traditional high

---

[1] For USAR, U.S. Army Recruiting Command (USAREC) recruits persons without prior military service and prior service–civil life gains (PS-CLG). The latter includes recruits who have met any Individual Ready Reserve obligation and have been out of the military for a period of time (e.g., more than six months).

[2] As described in Knapp et al. (2018, p. 1), "Recruiters, advertising, and enlistment bonuses offered to prospective recruits peaked in FY 2007–FY 2008. Because bonuses are paid upon completion of Initial Entry Training (IET)—and for bonuses over $10,000, the remainder is paid out over the recruit's term of enlistment—the actual costs incurred by the Army peaked in FY 2008–FY 2009."

school diplomas or who score below the fiftieth percentile on the Armed Forces Qualification Test (AFQT), the national average for the U.S. youth population.

Recruiting resources and enlistment eligibility policies work together as a system to produce RA and USAR recruits. Understanding their interactions under varying recruiting requirements and recruiting environments enables decisionmakers to use their limited resources more effectively and efficiently to achieve the Army's Active Duty and USAR accession requirements. The research detailed in this report builds on prior work by the RAND Arroyo Center on the effectiveness and lead times of alternative recruiting resources. It models the relationships among the monthly level and mix of recruiting resources, recruit eligibility policies, accumulated contracts, and unit vacancy targets, and models how these factors combine to produce monthly accessions.

The RRRM developed in this study consists of a contract production submodel and a cost allocation submodel, plus an optimization algorithm that generates solutions that minimize costs subject to accession goals and other constraints. The contract production submodel weighs trade-offs between recruiting requirements and conditions, on the one hand, and recruiting resources, on the other, in producing a specific number of total (overall) and high quality (HQ) enlistment contracts. As used in this report, HQ is defined using the Department of Defense standard of a traditional attendance-based high school diploma and a score in the upper fifty percentiles of the AFQT.[3] Based on the contract characteristics (e.g., HQ contracts) and unit vacancies (as represented by missioning), contracts are generated to fill units at a specific time.

The contract production model (CPM) reflects the relationship between contracts generated, the recruiting resources used, and the recruiting environment over the period of our data (2012–2018). The business model used during that period includes team recruiting rather than individual missioning and dual missioning of recruiting companies and stations to produce both RA and USAREC USAR contracts. The parameters of the RRRM CPM are estimated using data representing the recruiting environment, spending

---

[3]   In recent years, the U.S. Congress has allocated this Tier 1 status to homeschooled youth and those studying through distance learning technology.

on recruiting resources, USAREC missioning, and contracts generated by recruiting company and month. The model allows for diminishing returns in resources, including possible threshold and saturation effects for advertising. Whether greater contract production depends on resourcing, missioning, population, or the characteristics of recruiting companies is driven by the model's parameters. The estimated model indicates that enlistment contract production is sensitive to all recruiting resources: recruiters, bonuses, and television prospect advertising.

The cost allocation submodel estimates the recruiting resource costs paid to achieve the fiscal year's enlisted accessions. Some costs, such as advertising and recruiter costs, are paid regardless of contracting outcomes. However, enlistment incentive costs (bonuses) are paid out over time on a contract-by-contract basis. The cost allocation model accounts for costs when the Army becomes obligated to pay them—that is, in the month recruits sign enlistment contracts. Assessing costs at the contract production point permits creation of an optimization algorithm to identify strategically cost-minimizing resource portfolios.

The optimization algorithm used in the RRRM identifies the portfolio of recruiting resources that meets two objectives: (1) to produce enough accessions to fill each month's unit vacancies and total yearly mission, and (2) to minimize total costs. In our results, we discuss using the RRRM tool to predict annual accessions from a specified baseline resourcing plan (i.e., a nonoptimized outcome). We then provide several examples of how the RRRM tool can be used to assess potential recruiting resource and policy trade-offs or to prepare for alternative recruiting requirements via optimization of recruiting resources used for USAR recruiting. These examples include cost trade-offs based on

1. alternative accession goals
2. alternative recruit eligibility policies
3. alternative resourcing strategies.

These examples demonstrate important strategic-level trade-offs. The estimated CPM shows that USAR contracting outcomes are affected by RA mission: as RA mission increases, USAR contracts decline. Additionally, as the difficulty level of recruiting responds to changes in accession requirements, success and efficiency require different levels and mixes of recruiting resources and enlistment eligibility policies. Army planners can use the RRRM tool to assess the potential cost and resourcing requirements for varying recruiting contingencies. In our examples, the Army can save in excess of $100 million by optimizing the resource mix. Our excursions also show that changing recruit eligibility policies can lower recruiting resource requirements by hundreds of millions of dollars. Our alternative resource strategy example shows that emphasizing one resource over others (e.g., using enlistment bonuses reactively to deal with recruiting difficulties, as proxied by keeping recruiters and advertising levels fixed instead of proactively planning for such difficulties as proxied by optimizing over all resources) can cost substantially more or can lead to failure to achieve high recruiting missions. Moreover, using the RRRM tool in concert with the Reserve Recruit Selection Tool (described in unpublished RAND Corporation research) enables policymakers to consider first-term outcomes and costs associated with broadening eligibility policies in addition to savings in recruiting costs.

The RRRM tool informs Army planners and leaders about potential trade-offs in monthly recruiting resource levels and mixes given contemporaneous recruit eligibility policies and the recruiting environment. Using a mathematically based model with explicit assumptions and caveats, the RRRM tool identifies a cost-efficient strategy to achieve Army accession goals. The continued success of the RRRM tool requires maintaining the model so that it continues to reflect the effectiveness of recruiting resources. Future refinements include integration with the RA Recruiting Resource Model and with existing Army planning and budgeting models to account for the payment of bonus amounts in excess of $10,000 over time (as anniversary of enlistment payments distributed equally over the years of one's term) instead of costing bonuses in the year in which the commitment is made; this would make the RRRM tool a budgeting resource in addition to a strategic resource.

Acknowledgments

We are appreciative of the support of the sponsor of this project, Mark Davis, formerly the Deputy Assistant Secretary of the Army for Marketing, and his office, the former Army Marketing and Research Group, for their support of the research documented in this report, including John Jessup, Shawn McCurry, Alicia McCleary, Jeff Sterling, John Keeter, Jan Jedrych, MAJ Trent Geisler, Heather Whitehouse, and Terrance Mann. At Headquarters, Department of the Army, G-1, we are grateful for feedback at different phases of this project from then COL Joanne Moore, Mr. Roy Wallace, the Deputy, G-1, MAJ Larry Tobin, LTC Tom Kucik, CPT Eric O'Connor, and Dr. Bob Steinrauf. We also wish to express our thanks to COL Ken Burkman, Mike Nelson, Joe Baird, and Rick Ayer, currently or formerly at the U.S. Army Recruiting Command.

At the RAND Corporation, we would like to thank Christine DeMartini for her programming assistance and Chris Maerzluft for his technical expertise in tool development, as well as Jason Ward and Jeff Wenger for their help in developing the Reserve Recruiting Resource Model (RRRM).

We thank our peer reviewers, Molly McIntosh from RAND and Curtis Simon from Clemson University, as well as Michael Hansen from RAND, for their valuable reviews and comments. Finally, we thank David Knapp, formerly at RAND, for sharing his experience and knowledge of the development and use of the Regular Army Recruiting Resource Model and his earlier work on development of the RRRM with the research team.

Abbreviations

AFQT	Armed Forces Qualification Test
AMRG	Army Marketing and Research Group
COBYLA	Constrained Optimization by Linear Approximation
CPM	contract production model
DEP	Delayed Entry Program
DoDI	Department of Defense Instruction
FY	fiscal year
GRP	gross rating point
HQ	high quality
HQDA	Headquarters, Department of the Army
HRC	Human Resources Command
IET	Initial Entry Training
MOS	Military Occupational Specialty
NPS	non–prior service
ODCS	Office of the Deputy Chief of Staff
PS	prior service
PS-CLG	prior service–civil life gains
RA	Regular Army
RA RRM	Regular Army Recruiting Resource Model
RCM	recruiting contract month
RRRM	Reserve Recruiting Resource Model
USAR	U.S. Army Reserve
USAREC	U.S. Army Recruiting Command

CHAPTER ONE

Introduction

Background

Since 2001, between 57,000 and 80,000 enlisted soldiers per fiscal year have accessed into the Regular Army (RA) and 11,000 to 27,000 into the U.S. Army Reserve (USAR) through the U.S. Army Recruiting Command (USAREC). As a result, the U.S. Army's recruiting enterprise is substantial, with 9,000 recruiters placed at over 1,300 recruiting stations across the country (as of May 2017), a national advertising campaign directed by the Army Enterprise Management Office, and an enlistment incentive (i.e., bonus) structure historically managed at least quarterly by the Enlistment Incentive Review Board. In fiscal year (FY) 2008 and FY 2009, nearly $2.0 billion in 2020 dollars was spent per year on Army recruiting.[1] The average

---

[1] This estimate is intended to provide a sense of magnitude. It is based on marketing and incentive costs and recruiter numbers provided by the Office of the Deputy Chief of Staff (ODCS), G-1, within Headquarters, Department of the Army (HQDA): marketing, $328 million; enlistment incentives, $669 million; and recruiters, $944 million. The marketing and enlistment incentives are inflated by the U.S. Bureau of Labor Statistics' Consumer Price Index–Urban Consumers to 2020 dollars; recruiter costs reflect the average cost per recruiter based on the most recent estimate provided to us ($111,324 per recruiter in 2018) by HQDA. Due to normal manning issues and USAREC's operational requirements, the number of recruiters on duty likely differs from the required recruiting force. Enlistment incentives involve both payments for current enlistments and anniversary payments for large bonuses due to prior enlistees, not the bonus amounts obligated to contracts written during the year of contract execution. Recruiting resource spending peaked in FY 2007–FY 2008. However, because bonuses over $10,000 include anniversary payments over the recruit's term of enlistment for the amount over $10,000, the Army's actual costs peaked in FY 2008–FY 2009.

for the period FY 2001–FY 2014 was $1.6 billion per year in 2020 dollars. The average annual cost of a USAR accession, accounting only for recruiters, bonuses, and television advertising for prospects spending for which we have data, ranged from $56,500 (FY 2013) to $94,200 (FY 2018) in nominal dollars, with the average cost for FY 2013–FY 2018 being $70,300.[2] Cost differences reflect variation in both recruiting environments and the accession mission. Previous research shows that when difficult environments and large missions occur simultaneously, as during FY 2005–FY 2008, the marginal cost of a recruiting contract can be much greater than the average cost of the enlistment contracts produced (Knapp et al., 2018).

Recruiting resources differ both in their cost per additional contract produced and in the lead time required between resource use and enlistment supply response. Enlistment bonuses can have the most immediate impact, but they are relatively expensive. Adding recruiters or increasing advertising is less costly, but these recruiting resources involve more planning time and more time to increase the number of enlistment contracts. Unit vacancies occur unevenly across the fiscal year, adding another element for Army planners to consider. Resourcing needs to be planned with enough lead time such that contracts are produced to ensure that enlistees fill unit vacancies.

Resource levels and mix are not the sole policy levers the Army uses to achieve its recruiting mission. Rather, it uses a suite of recruiting resources and recruit eligibility policies. Department of Defense Instruction (DoDI) 1145.01 specifies benchmarks for potential recruit eligibility, including 60 percent of fiscal year accessions scoring in the upper fifty percentiles of the Armed Forces Qualification Test (AFQT) national U.S. youth population distribution and 90 percent traditional high school graduates with

---

[2] This estimate is provided to give the reader a sense of magnitude of the realized expenditures in the data used herein, allowing for a comparison of optimized and nonoptimized partial recruiting costs. Data were provided by the Army Marketing and Research Group (AMRG); the ODCS, G-1; and the U.S. Army Human Resources Command (HRC). Figures are presented in nominal dollars. Recruiter costs are based on the average cost ($111,324 per recruiter) provided by HQDA. Bonus figures reflect the aggregation of contract-level bonus information in the administrative data. We note that recruiters and advertising dollars also contribute to RA accessions.

diplomas earned through attendance (DoDI 1145.01, 2013, p. 2).[3] Consistent with Office of the Secretary of Defense practice, this report refers to enlistees with both of these characteristics as high quality (HQ) enlistees.

DoDI 1304.26 establishes additional qualifications for enlistments related to other factors, including medical condition, physical fitness, conduct, and drug and alcohol use (DoDI 1304.26, 1993, pp. 6–12). It also establishes criteria for providing waivers based on current or past medical, conduct, and drug issues. The issuance of waivers is determined by the individual services. Although Army recruiting typically focuses on non–prior service (NPS) recruits, HQDA regularly establishes Prior Service Business Rules concerning the ability of recruiters to enlist individuals with prior service (PS). Recruits into USAR with PS can affiliate directly when leaving active duty, from the Individual Ready Reserve, shortly after leaving active duty, or later as Prior Service-Civil Life Gains (PS-CLG). USAREC's PS recruiting *mission*, however, involves *only* PS-CLG.

As with recruiting resources, recruit eligibility can be expanded during difficult recruiting conditions and contracted at other times. For example, and despite the benchmarks set in DoDI 1145.01, between FY 2003 and FY 2018, the share of HQ recruits among all recruits (NPS plus PS-CLG contracts) for USAR has varied between 23 and 67 percent. Among NPS contracts alone, the HQ share ranges from 32 to 89 percent on a month-to-month basis. Over this same period, the share of contracts (across NPS and PS-CLG) with any type of waiver varied on average from about 3 percent to just over 10 percent. Expanding recruit eligibility can substantially reduce the cost of achieving recruiting goals and reduce the risk of mission failure.

In different recruiting environments, the relative utility of alternative recruiting resource and enlistment eligibility policies in meeting accession requirements varies. There is a strong association between the tightening of the external labor market (i.e., the civilian unemployment rate decreases) and the ability of USAREC to meet its monthly RA contract mission (Knapp et al., 2018; Wenger et al., 2019). This report estimates the effect of a tightening of the labor market on the USAR contract mission.

---

[3] Congress has included homeschooled youth and those completing high school through distance learning in recent years. They make up a limited percentage of youth in the Tier 1 education category.

The Purpose of This Report

Understanding how recruiting resources and recruit eligibility policies work together under varying accession requirements and recruiting environments is critical in enabling decisionmakers to use limited resources to efficiently and effectively meet the Army's accession mission. This research builds on earlier research, including that conducted by the RAND Arroyo Center, on the effectiveness of and lead times required by alternative recruiting resources in generating enlistment contracts and accessions. The Reserve Recruiting Resource Model (RRRM) developed here considers the relationship among the monthly level and mix of recruiting resources, recruit eligibility policies, and unit vacancy targets. It models how these factors combine to produce monthly accessions and produces estimates of the minimum resource requirements necessary to meet USAR recruiting goals. The RRRM and its companion, the Regular Army Recruiting Resource Model (RA RRM), are suitable for planning at the strategic recruiting and budgeting level.

Our Approach

The RRRM consists of two components, or submodels, and an algorithm that solves for least-cost solutions of meeting the recruiting mission. The first component is the contract production model (CPM), which uses a regression approach to estimate the relationship between recruiting resources, objectives (mission), and the recruiting environment on total contracts and USAR HQ NPS contracts.[4] The second component is the cost allocation model, which parameterizes the costs of using various recruiting resources. The RRRM uses these two components and an optimization routine to solve for the least-cost resource use given an assumed monthly mission, quality mix, and various constraints that reflect operational realities.

The CPM reflects the Army's recruiting business practices from the end of FY 2012 to FY 2018, and is estimated using Army and economic data that indicate the recruiting environment, spending on recruiting resources, and

---

[4] PS-CLG contracts are passed to the model as a user assumption.

USAREC missioning by recruiting company and month. The CPM specification allows diminishing returns for recruiting resources, including possible threshold and saturation effects for advertising. For instance, if there is no recruiter at a recruiting station, that station has no USAR contract mission, or no youth live within the recruiting station's geographic bounds, the CPM would not include the station in its recruiting company's results and it would yield no USAR contracts. Recruiting companies with more youth in their geographic footprints may produce more enlistment contracts, and persistent differences may exist among regions based on unobserved factors such as different average propensity to enlist. The model's parameters, which are estimated using detailed data, take these and other differences into account and determine the extent to which resourcing, missioning, population, or the properties of recruiting companies are associated with greater contract production. The CPM was validated in-sample through correlation and graphical analysis, in addition to standard model fit statistics.

Some costs in the cost allocation submodel, such as advertising and recruiter costs, are realized regardless of the number of contracts ultimately generated. However, other costs, such as enlistment incentives, are determined as a function of the number of contracts signed. The cost allocation model assesses costs when the Army becomes *obligated* to pay them—for example, the month the enlistee signs the contract or the month a television commercial is first broadcast. This enables creation of an optimization algorithm to identify cost-minimizing resource portfolios.

The cost-minimizing portfolio of recruiting resources is conditional on the recruiting environment and recruit eligibility policies. The optimization algorithm has two objectives: (1) to produce enough accessions to fill each month's unit vacancies, and (2) to minimize total costs. We refer to the combination of the RRRM and the optimization algorithm as the RRRM tool. We provide examples of how the RRRM tool can be used, including predicting execution year accessions from a specified resourcing plan (i.e., a nonoptimized outcome), and three optimized outcomes. These examples include cost trade-offs based on

1. alternative accession goals
2. alternative recruit eligibility policies
3. alternative resourcing strategies.

The RRRM tool can help Army leaders understand the complex trade-offs involved in recruiting. The RRRM can be refined to reflect changes in the effectiveness and efficiency of individual recruiting resources, USAREC company structure or operations, and lessons learned about the results of changes in recruit eligibility policies.

The Organization of the Report

Chapter Two discusses use of recruiting resources and enlistment eligibility policies and the recruiting environment since FY 2003, as well as prior enlistment supply research. Chapter Three discusses the data used in our analysis, as well as past measures of enlistment supply's responsiveness to recruiting resources and the recruiting environment. Chapter Four provides an overview of the model and a detailed discussion of the two model components. Chapter Five discusses how the optimization algorithm works and provides three examples of using the RRRM tool to examine the effects of increased recruiting missions and trade-offs involved using expanded recruit eligibility and alternative resourcing policies. Chapter Six contains our conclusions and recommendations.

CHAPTER TWO

An Overview of Past Resource Use and Eligibility Policies

In this chapter we discuss accession goals and the recruiting environment since FY 2003.[1] We next describe how recruiting resources and recruit eligibility policies were used in attempting to meet the accession goals.[2] We focus on major resource and policy levers that were used during this period. In the last portion of the chapter we review prior research on enlistment supply and discuss how the RRRM fits within this body of research.

Recruiting Goals and Environment

From 2003 to 2018, RA accession goals ranged from 57,000 to 80,000 enlisted accessions per year; USAREC USAR missions varied from 11,000 to 27,000 per year. During this period, the RA missed its accession goal only twice, in 2005 and 2018. When RA recruiting is more challenging than expected, recruiters may have an incentive to divert effort away from USAR

---

[1] In this report we use recruiting and accession goals interchangeably, since there is no Delayed Entry Program (DEP) for USAR; given attrition during the DEP process, this is not appropriate for the RA.

[2] FY 2003 was the first fiscal year for which we collected complete Army data for recruiters, missioning, and contracts.

recruiting and toward RA recruiting because RA shortfalls may be viewed as more costly. During such times, policymakers may have an incentive to increase enlistment bonuses or offer additional incentives to enlist in the RA; to the extent that those factors are not perfectly measured, there may be substitution on the part of the individual recruit between RA and USAR enlistment choices. Indeed, USAREC missed its USAR recruiting goal by more than 4,000 recruits in 2005 and 2018 (equivalent to 16 and 21 percent, respectively).

The times that the RA missed its accession goals were characterized by low U.S. adult population unemployment rates (between 4 and 5 percent); increased accession goals (80,000 in FY 2005 and an in-year increase to 68,500 in FY 2017); and a higher goal for HQ recruits in the year the accession mission was missed, followed by a lower percentage of HQ recruits in the years immediately following the missed recruiting goals in the FY 2005–FY 2008 time frame. This pattern suggests that relaxing eligibility restrictions to deal with a worsening recruiting environment happened too late. The relaxation of eligibility criteria is primarily reflected in the decrease in Tier 1 (mainly attendance-based high school graduate) enlistments from FY 2006 to FY 2008, whose percentages got as low as the low 70s. By contrast, Tier 1 enlistment rates in FY 2017 and FY 2018 were 95.8 and 95.0 percent, respectively (Gilroy et al., 2020; Knapp et al., 2018).

Table 2.1 shows the programmed and achieved USAR accessions for USAR overall, NPS contracts, total PS contracts (including PS-CLG contracts and all others), and USAREC PS contracts (only PS-CLG contracts). Shortfalls relative to mission are indicated by bold text on actual accessions. Of note, USAREC failed to achieve its USAR mission by substantial amounts for the periods FY 2005–FY 2006 and FY 2013–FY 2018 (except for FY 2016). The latter period was essentially one of steadily declining unemployment following the Great Recession. Furthermore, all of the missed total USAR accession years were associated with NPS shortfalls, with only FY 2010 exhibiting NPS shortfalls overcome by PS contracts.

Figure 2.1 shows the quality data for NPS USAR contracts over the FY 2003–FY 2018 period. As noted above with respect to the RA, the period

TABLE 2.1

U.S. Army Reserve Programmed Mission and Realized Enlisted Accessions (FY 2003–FY 2018)

FY	USAR Mission	Achieved USAR Accessions	NPS Mission	USAREC NPS Actual	Total PS Mission	Total PS Achieved	USAREC PS Mission	USAREC PS Actual
2003	40,900	41,851	21,200	22,579	19,700	19,272	5,200	**4,786**
2004	32,275	32,699	16,200	16,648	16,075	**16,051**	5,000	**4,630**
2005	28,485	**23,859**	18,175	**12,906**	10,310	10,953	4,000	4,880
2006	36,032	**34,379**	20,000	**16,546**	16,032	17,833	5,500	**5,081**
2007	35,505	35,736	19,000	19,832	16,505	**15,904**	6,000	**4,592**
2008	37,500	39,870	21,000	22,909	16,500	16,961	5,500	**4,034**
2009	34,144	36,181	19,000	19,566	15,144	16,615	3,500	4,105
2010	26,000	26,471	13,000	**12,916**	13,000	13,555	4,000	**3,786**
2011	28,000	29,692	15,000	16,228	13,000	13,464	4,000	**3,380**
2012	26,555	**25,769**	13,430	**12,937**	13,125	**12,832**	2,250	2,522
2013	29,560	**26,314**	17,810	**13,668**	11,750	12,646	2,000	**1,772**
2014	29,000	**26,709**	15,500	**13,147**	13,500	13,562	2,500	**1,342**
2015	27,500	**26,570**	14,500	**13,910**	13,000	**12,660**	2,500	**1,061**
2016	25,500	26,082	14,000	14,769	11,500	**11,313**	1,000	**991**
2017	23,845	**22,811**	13,000	**12,369**	10,845	**10,442**	1,500	**790**
2018	24,180	**19,189**	14,580	**10,531**	9,600	**8,658**	800	**672**

SOURCE: Data provided to the authors by the Office of the Chief of the Army Reserve, G-1.

NOTES: "USAREC PS Mission" column indicates PS-CLG accessions. Boldfaced numbers denote shortfalls within a category.

FY 2006–FY 2008 saw a dip in both Tier 1 and the upper fifty percentiles of the AFQT, but since FY 2012 both measures have remained fairly steady (with the exception of FY 2014). It does not appear that USAR relaxed quality standards during the recent years of the data when it missed mission, consistent with relaxing standards too late.

FIGURE 2.1

Percentage of Tier 1, Upper Fifty Percentiles of the Armed Forces Qualification Test, and U.S. Army Reserve High Quality Contracts (FY 2003–FY 2018, monthly)

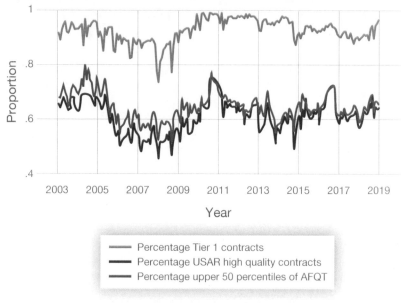

SOURCE: This information is derived from administrative data from the USAHRC and USAREC, as described in Chapter Three.

Recruiting Resources

In this report we focus on three recruiting resources: recruiters, enlistment bonuses, and advertising. Recruiters are assigned to stations, which belong to recruiting companies, the next higher organizational echelon. Figure 2.2 shows changes in USAREC companies and stations from FY 2003 to FY 2018. After the Army failed its accession mission in FY 2005, a significant number of additional recruiters were added. The number of recruiters remained relatively constant through FY 2007, after which time more recruiters were placed at stations. The number of recruiters at stations in the 50 states and the District of Columbia peaked in June 2009. The recruiting environment then improved and accession goals were reduced, which led to a reduction in the number of recruiters. Beginning in the fourth quarter of FY 2011,

FIGURE 2.2

U.S. Army Reserve Recruiters and Recruiting Companies and Stations (FY 2003–FY 2018)

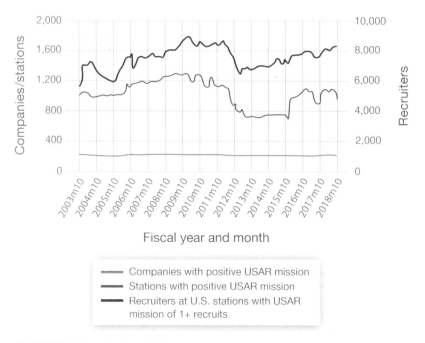

Companies with positive USAR mission
Stations with positive USAR mission
Recruiters at U.S. stations with USAR mission of 1+ recruits

SOURCE: This information is derived from administrative data provided by USAREC, as described in Chapter Three.

NOTES: Companies and stations reflect locations within the 50 states and the District of Columbia where at least one recruiter is assigned and the location is assigned a production mission of one or more recruits; "Recruiters" reflects recruiters assigned to such locations. The time series is for RCMs for the fiscal year. Recruiting calendar months are divided into recruiting periods called phase-lines and recruit ship months. In this report, we refer to the phase line periods as recruiting contract months, that is, the days during a month-long period when enlistment contracts can be signed for that phase line period. As discussed in the report, phase-line periods run from the middle of one month to the middle of the next. Recruit ship months indicate the last day within a month to ship recruits for the corresponding phase line period.

USAREC consolidated its operations primarily within recruiting companies by reducing the number of stations and recruiters.[3] Since that time, however, the number of recruiters has increased, though there have been some periods of temporary decline.

---

[3] The geographic boundaries (footprint) of recruiting companies and stations change over time. Such changes were more common during the FY 2012 time frame.

FIGURE 2.3

U.S. Army Reserve Enlistment Bonus Receipt and Bonus Levels (FY 2003–FY 2018)

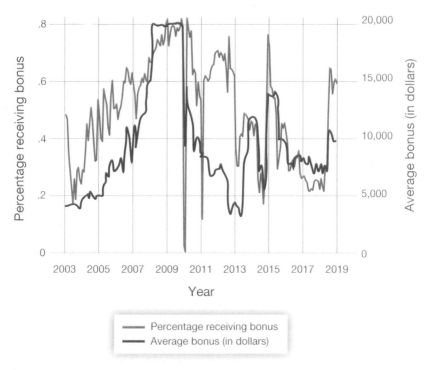

SOURCE: This information is derived from administrative data from USAHRC and USAREC, as described in Chapter Three.

NOTES: Average bonus levels reflect the average bonus of contracts signed in a recruiting contract month (RCM) conditional on receipt of a Military Occupational Specialty (MOS) bonus. These values are reported in current-year dollars. The fraction receiving the bonus is calculated based on all contracts signed in an RCM. The realized bonus level may reflect additional bonus categories for which an enlistee is qualified. The time series is for RCMs for the fiscal year.

The Army sharply expanded both the fraction of recruits receiving and the dollar amount per recruit of enlistment bonuses between FY 2003 and FY 2010 from 20 percent to nearly 80 percent. As the recruiting environment improved, enlistment bonus use contracted to around 30 percent, although a couple of positive spikes are visible in FY 2015 and FY 2018.

The unit of observation in our analysis is the recruiting company. Although data on the number of recruiters and on enlistment bonus receipt are readily aggregated to the company level, determining the quantity of advertising at that level is complex, requires a number of simplifying assumptions, and involves several intermediate steps (for more detail, see Chapter Three).[4] Figure 2.4 shows the data used in this study from FY 2012 through FY 2018. Monthly television prospect advertising expenditures peaked at $15 million during certain months in FY 2015 and FY 2016, but average just under $5 million in the last months of the data. This corresponds to annual expenditures ranging from about $15 million in FY 2012 to a peak of $64 million in FY 2016.

FIGURE 2.4

Television Prospect Advertising Spending (FY 2013–FY 2018)

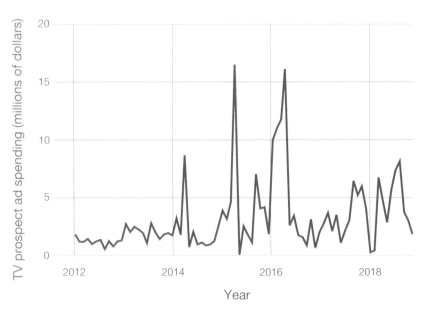

SOURCE: This information is derived from data from the AMRG, the HQDA, and the Army's former advertising agency.
NOTE: The time series is for RCMs for the fiscal year in nominal dollars.

---

[4] DD804-4, a required report to Congress, provides the closest consistently collected data for advertising. It categorizes the services' recruiting resource spending into various measures, including television advertising. The data are, however, reported only at the national level, and only annually, and combine advertising across submarkets (e.g., Army medical advertising).

Recruit Eligibility Policies

There are two major eligibility policy levers that can increase accessions and that have been used in the past, especially when the recruiting environment is difficult: increased waiver use (for medical and conduct waivers) and reductions in the proportion of HQ accessions. We discuss each in turn.

Enlistment waivers can be required for a variety of reasons, but the two types that have been most commonly granted are medical and nondrug misdemeanor conduct waivers. Figure 2.5 shows the monthly variation in medical and conduct waivers by contract month and year. The use of these waivers increased substantially after FY 2005, and remained high through

FIGURE 2.5

U.S. Army Reserve Medical and Conduct Waivers (FY 2003–FY 2018)

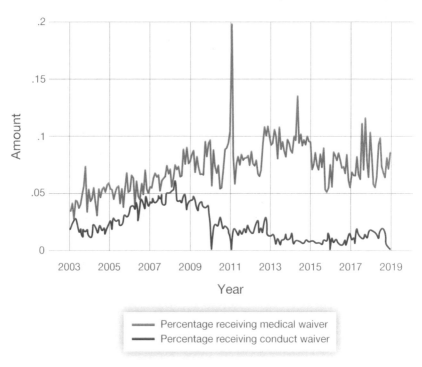

SOURCE: This information is derived from administrative data from USAHRC and USAREC, as described in Chapter Three.
NOTE: The time series is for recruiting contract months for the fiscal year.

FY 2009, after which the conduct waiver percentage declined while medical waivers stayed at a relatively high, but variable, percentage. Across all fiscal years, medical waivers are more commonly granted than conduct waivers, with the average in the available data showing a 2.1-percent waiver rate for conduct and a 7.1-percent medical waiver rate.

Analogously, HQ goals have been lowered during difficult recruiting conditions in order to increase enlistment supply. We show annual variation in HQ enlistments in Figure 2.6. In FY 2005, quality goals were notably reduced, likely reflecting an effort to meet accession goals. Quality marks remained low from FY 2006 to FY 2008 in both the RA and USAR, partly through an agreement with the Office of the Secretary of Defense involving the use of the Tier 2 Attrition Screen developed by the Army Research Institute to screen in an additional 10 percent of recruits who held Tier 2

FIGURE 2.6

U.S. Army Reserve High Quality U.S. Army Reserve Contracts (FY 2003–FY 2018)

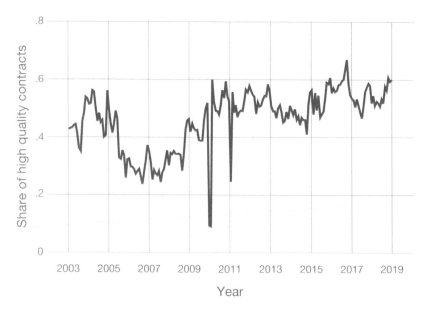

SOURCE: This information is derived from administrative data from USAHRC and USAREC, as described in Chapter Three.
NOTE: The time series is for RCMs for the fiscal year.

education credentials (essentially, general equivalency diploma holders) who passed the Tier 2 Attrition Screen and were in AFQT categories I–IIIA. In some months, the percentage of HQ contracts dropped below 40 percent, before rising during FY 2009 and FY 2010 as recruiting improved. Since that time, through FY 2018 they have averaged just under 60 percent, with some year-to-year variation.

Related Research

As documented in Knapp et al. (2018), research on enlistment supply prior to 2012 has assessed how accessions change with changes in education incentives, enlistment bonuses, advertising, and recruiters, but generally did not deal with recruit eligibility policies (examples include Asch et al., 2010; Asch, Hosek, and Warner, 2007; Dertouzos, 2009; Dertouzos and Garber, 2003; and Warner, Simon, and Payne, 2001, 2003). Most of these studies used data on the RA at the national level, focused on HQ recruits, and as such are subject to some fairly extensive endogeneity problems (i.e., measuring net correlations in resource use and contracts rather than the structural parameter that explains supply response to a change in resource use). One exception is the analysis of the Enlistment Bonus Experiment, which used variation in recruiting regions to independently vary bonuses from the rest of the recruiting environment (Polich, Dertouzos, and Press, 1986).

Arkes and Kilburn (2005) modeled USAR enlistments across all services using data from 1992 through 1999 at the state level using econometric methods. In particular, for their NPS models they modeled the ratio of number of accessions into USAR to the predicted values of the number of 18-year-olds in the state and the ratio of number of accessions into the RA to the number of 18-year-olds in the state. They use a similar form for HQ accessions and also model PS contracts. They find that for the time period under consideration (prior to team recruiting), the RA and USAR were competing for the same resources. They also find that increases in the unemployment rate were associated with increases in both RA and USAR contracting, as well as significant results related to the share of minority population in a state and the cost of college. Finally, the authors recognized that their estimates suffered from endogeneity problems but found stability in the model coefficients.

It is important to update models of enlistment supply so that they represent current circumstances. The effectiveness of a recruiting resource can change over time; for example, when the Post-9/11 GI Bill took effect in 2009, the Army College Fund, which had been a highly cost-effective enlistment option, became largely irrelevant since it added little to the benefits under the new GI Bill. Army recruiter effort effects have changed as USAREC changed from individual recruiter missioning to team recruiting wherein missions are assigned to stations and companies. Such changes can also affect the estimated productivity of enlistment bonuses. Enlistment bonuses were offered as a stand-alone option or in competition or combination with education incentives in the 1990s. Recruiter write rates (the number of contracts a recruiter writes monthly) also decreased after 2001.

Our project is most similar to Knapp et al. (2018), with the RRRM being a direct extension of the RA model presented therein. That previous report did not explore USAR accessions, used data only through FY 2015 (the most recent then available), and used a slightly different econometric specification (for more details, see "Innovations in the Reserve Recruiting Resource Model" in Chapter Four). This report should be considered a direct complement to that work. The Arkes and Kilburn (2005) report was based on data from over two decades prior to the writing of the present report, and thus we would not necessarily expect for all of the relationships estimated therein to hold for the more recent data set. In fact, even our use of television prospect advertising may be slightly dated given changes in the media environment. In the future, we plan to incorporate the relationships between internet and social media advertising and enlistment.

Overall, prior research has investigated the role of bonuses (including enlistment bonuses), incentives, advertising, and recruiters, usually using RA data with models estimated from data at the national level that varies over time. This research provides guidance as to the important variables to include in the contract production functions. Relatively little past work has been done to estimate these relationships for the reserve components, but the work done suggests that the RA and USAR compete for recruiting resources, and that the USAR tends to increase realized enlistees when civilian job opportunities decline. These are testable hypotheses for the current research. Finally, endogeneity issues are a prevalent problem in this type of research given the structure of the available data. In Knapp et al. (2018) and the present report, the endogeneity issues were partially addressed through estimation at the company-month level, and in this report we add a flexible time trend polynomial that may help to control for unobservable variables that would otherwise contaminate the error term of the contract production function. However, in both reports it is likely that some issues remain, potentially biasing the coefficients.

CHAPTER THREE

Data Used for This Study

Data were collected from several sources and were categorized into three types: Army data, television advertising data, and economic and demographic data. This information is organized into a data set at the recruiting company-month level (i.e., a panel with a company-level cross-sectional dimension and monthly time dimension) following the procedures documented below and in Knapp et al. (2018). Because television advertising is only available starting in FY 2012, our full data set covered the period September 2012–September 2018. The following sections review the data and provide additional technical notes about data set construction.

Army Data

We drew data largely from databases maintained by the USAHRC; the ODCS, G-1; the Office of the Chief of the Army Reserve, G-1; and USAREC.

Recruiters' current status and assignment were available via a database maintained by USAREC. The database contains monthly snapshots for each recruiter, including his or her company and station assignment and whether he or she is actively pursuing recruiting goals that month (as compared with being on leave or assigned to some other duty assignment). The database covers August 2002–September 2018.

Missioning data were collected from a database maintained by USAREC that reports enlistment contract mission goals and achievements. Key measures are recorded at the recruiting brigade, battalion, company, and station levels, and can be used to generate a monthly time series of missioning objectives for particular categories of recruits, such as graduate alphas (high school graduate AFQT category I–IIIAs), senior alphas (i.e., high school senior I–IIIAs), and others (i.e., neither graduate alphas nor senior alphas) in both the RA and USAR.[1]

Using the missioning and recruiter data, we calculated the number of recruiters "on production" at the station level by adding together the number of recruiters at stations with missions of at least one USAR contract and calculated the monthly HQ contract mission by adding together the mission with at least one graduate alpha or senior alpha contract and at least one recruiter on production at the station.[2] Attention was restricted to recruiting stations in the 50 states and the District of Columbia. RA monthly mission was calculated in an identical manner. We used positive missioning information to control for the opening and closing of stations; that can falsely increase the estimated mission assigned in a month. Station-level data were then aggregated to the company level.

Enlistment contract information was collected from USAR Analyst files maintained by the USAHRC. The files covered all contracts written beginning in FY 2001. Key measures for these contracts included when the contract was written, the recruiter responsible for it, the total amount and types of bonuses included in the contract, the education level and Armed Services Vocational Aptitude Battery scores of the recruit, and the projected and actual accession dates for the recruit, among other variables.[3] We used this information to calculate key monthly contract measures, including the proportion of recruits receiving each type of enlistment bonus at the national level, total contracts written at the company level, and the number of contracts written for specific subgroups (e.g., HQ recruits) at the company level. We again limited the sample to contracts written in the 50 states or the District of Columbia at stations with at least one recruiter on production and with a contract mission of at least one.

---

[1] USAREC gives a monthly recruiting mission to each brigade. The brigades allocate contract missions to their battalions, the battalions allocate contract missions to their companies, and the companies in turn allocate contract missions to their stations.

[2] In some fiscal years, the recording of missioning at the station level is inconsistent. In these cases we use missioning at the company level.

[3] In the USAR analyst file, the contract date equals the projected accession date in a significant majority of cases, as accession is assumed to take place when a contract is signed.

Data on accession goals planned for future months were collected from the ODCS, G-1's accession mission letter. The mission letter provides both quality and total accession targets, though the quality goals in the mission letter seldom change. Therefore, we used only the accession mission from the letter. The mission letter is released at least annually to set the next fiscal year's targets. An updated mission letter may be issued with revised monthly targets if the accession mission changes or if projected accessions are too high or too low relative to the original targets for the fiscal year. The mission is based on unit vacancies.

Television Advertising Data

To investigate the relationship between advertising and contract production, we used data on national-level television advertising, which represented about 71 percent of Army media expenditures during our analysis period.[4] National advertising differs from local advertising in that (1) it is purchased from national media networks, and (2) the purchases guarantee a minimum number of national impressions (views). Purchases do not guarantee a number of local impressions (though both national and local television advertising do generate local impressions). Data were provided by the AMRG and the Army's former advertising agency.

Advertising data typically have three forms: planned, purchased, and actual. When purchases are made can differ from when the commercials are aired; this is based on network billing cycles. Our analysis matched purchases to the dates that commercials are aired and to the realized marketing impressions for the commercials aired in a particular subgeography as measured by an independent media analytics service. In other words, we focused on actual television advertising cost, excluding fixed costs linked to the Army's marketing contract, costs of marketing events, local advertising, and internet advertising, at a spatially disaggregated level.

In particular, we collected two types of television advertising data: impressions and costs. The number of impressions was calculated from

---

[4] Occasionally, local television advertising may be placed by a USAREC recruiting organization (i.e., a battalion, company, or station), but data on impressions and spending were not available for this activity.

gross rating points (GRPs) and population size.[5] The GRP measures viewership; it is calculated differently for each media market, and subpopulations have their own GRP measures. GRP measures include Local People Meter, Set Meter, and diary markets. Local People Meter markets collect viewership information continuously from the people in households that have had television watching meters installed. Set Meter markets collect information continuously from households; they use separate diaries of a week's viewing behavior for everyone in a sample of households. Diary markets rely on one-week diaries for viewership behavior; they are more often used in smaller media markets. Diaries are collected four times a year: in February, May, July, and November; these times are known as sweeps periods.

The Army's target subpopulations for advertising include prospects (men of ages 18–24) and influencers (all adults of ages 35–54). Advertising campaigns targeting each subpopulation have different goals. *Prospect campaigns* are intended to increase awareness about an Army career among potential recruits. In contrast, *influencer campaigns* are intended to generate awareness about the Army among a population largely ineligible to enlist. Because the prospect and influencer campaigns have different focuses, we use only television prospect impressions, which have the most direct effect, theoretically, on enlistment contract production.

We worked with AMRG and the Army's former advertising agency to generate local impressions for the prospect subpopulation based on detailed information about Army advertising in FY2012–FY 2018 and the three types of GRP measures. National impression estimates were generated using the continuous collection data, and local media market impressions were estimated using each year's November sweeps week measures (subpopulation sizes are also measured during sweep weeks).[6] Recruiting company areas were defined using the recruiting station identification code and data for ZIP codes covered by the recruiting station identification code. For data such as television advertising that is collected for geographic areas larger than ZIP codes (such as designated marketing areas), we use population

---

[5] The function is Impressions = (GRP/100) × Population Size. Thus, given an advertising campaign resulting in 20 percent of the target market seeing the advertising four times on average, the overall effect is 80 GRPs, or 0.8 impressions per person.

[6] The February sweeps period was used in lieu of November's for FY 2013, because the November data for the New York media market were not available.

shares from the 2010 U.S. Census to generate a weighted average for the recruiting company geography.

To make the projections, the Army's advertising agency used a tool provided by a third-party media analytics company. The impressions were used to allocate advertising spending to each local media market in accordance with their impression shares. We presented the national-level prospect television spending data used in the model in Figure 2.4. For more information about television prospect advertising and the underlying data, readers are referred to Knapp et al. (2018).

Economic and Demographic Data

Recruiting varies with economic differences and population size. We therefore included economic and demographic factors in the RRRM model, including qualified military population, local unemployment rates, the University of Michigan's Consumer Sentiment Index, the civilian-to-military wage ratio, and the local minimum wage. We used Woods and Poole Economics' projections of the qualified military available population by ZIP code based on U.S. Census population data as our primary measure of the enlistment-eligible population. Qualified military available youth are U.S. citizens 17–24 years of age who are eligible and available for enlisted military service without a waiver. Ineligibility is based on the following criteria:

- medical/physical condition
- risk of obesity
- mental health
- drug abuse
- conduct
- number of dependents
- aptitude.[7]

---

[7] Estimates of the qualified military available population are calculated by applying prior enlistment rejection rates to the military available population for the geographical area, using data from Joint Advertising Market Research & Studies Youth Poll surveys; the Military Entrance Processing Command Production Applicants AFQT Score Database; the National Health and Nutrition Examination Survey; the National Survey on Drug Use and Health; the 1997 Profile of American Youth; and Woods and Poole Economics' Population Estimates. See Joint Advertising Market Research & Studies (2016).

Unemployment rates are assessed using the Current Population Survey, a household survey administered monthly by the U.S. Census Bureau that employs the official definition of unemployment. The U.S. Bureau of Labor Statistics computes these measures and on a monthly basis projects county-level unemployment rates.

We use the University of Michigan's Consumer Sentiment Index to represent forward-looking opinions on the evolution of the economic environment. The Consumer Sentiment Index was devised in the late 1940s as a way to generate a meaningful empirical measure of how the attitudes and expectations of consumers influence economic activity. The intent of this measure is to acknowledge the powerful effect that beliefs among individuals have on influencing macroeconomic conditions (e.g., high expectations of future inflation will lead consumers to spend today if they believe incomes will not keep up with prices). For more details on this measure, see Curtin (2007).

The civilian-to-military wage ratio was constructed by the authors from data from two different sources. The civilian data came from tabulations of ZIP code tabulation area–level personal income for men with a high school diploma using American Community Survey five-year data sets where, for example, 2010–2014 was used for 2014 (so that this represents a moving average of past-to-present income estimates). Regular military compensation was taken from various volumes of the Department of Defense's *Compensation Greenbook* (U.S. Department of Defense, undated) using the "all military personnel" value.

The minimum wage data is the "State Minimum Wage Data Set through Sept. 2019" from David Neumark at the University of California–Irvine, and contains monthly data on each state's minimum wage dating back to 1960 (Neumark, undated).

Additional Technical Notes

Generally speaking, the data used in estimation correspond to the recruiting resources, enlistment eligibility policies, and economic conditions in effect in each calendar month from FY 2012 to FY 2018. Not all data correspond to calendar months, however. Enlistment contract-related measures are measured in RCMs; they normally cover the middle of the previous calendar month to the middle of the current month. The modeling must deal with this difference, since some measures are recorded using only one type of monthly measure. For example, enlistment contracts are missioned by RCM, while national economic measures are provided by calendar month, normally reflecting outcome measures from surveys administered during that month. To reconcile, all data reported for the calendar month is converted to RCM by lagging one month; that is, if an RCM covers the last half of February and the first half of March (the March RCM), the calendar-year data for February are assigned to that RCM. We account for the length of the RCM in the explanatory variables of the CPM.

CHAPTER FOUR

The Reserve Recruiting Resource Model

The RRRM is similar in structure to the RA RRM presented in Knapp et al. (2018) but is adapted to USAR. One significant difference is the lack of the DEP for USAR, thus rendering the DEP retention submodel irrelevant for the RRRM. But both the RA RRM and RRRM are designed to model how resources and policies that are set by the Army for USAR produce contracts in a particular recruiting environment and optimizing over the financial resources that are used to produce those contracts. Figure 4.1 shows the design of the RRRM.

The resources over which the RRRM optimizes remains the number of recruiters, television advertising, and enlistment incentives, though the vast

FIGURE 4.1
The Design of the Reserve Recruiting Resource Model

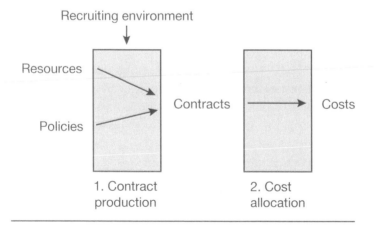

CHAPTER FOUR

The Reserve Recruiting Resource Model

The RRRM is similar in structure to the RA RRM presented in Knapp et al. (2018) but is adapted to USAR. One significant difference is the lack of the DEP for USAR, thus rendering the DEP retention submodel irrelevant for the RRRM. But both the RA RRM and RRRM are designed to model how resources and policies that are set by the Army for USAR produce contracts in a particular recruiting environment and optimizing over the financial resources that are used to produce those contracts. Figure 4.1 shows the design of the RRRM.

The resources over which the RRRM optimizes remains the number of recruiters, television advertising, and enlistment incentives, though the vast

FIGURE 4.1
The Design of the Reserve Recruiting Resource Model

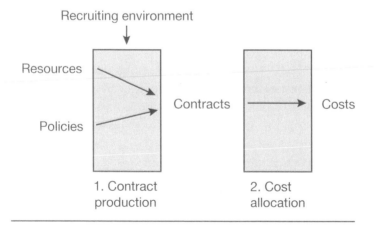

27

majority of USAR bonuses are based on MOS, and quick-ship bonuses are rarely used (unlike in the RA). Assuming budget is available, bonuses are under direct control of the Army and can be used to relatively quickly augment contracting. Television prospect advertising can be changed as well, though lead times are longer than for bonuses and the effects may be more indirect. Changing recruiters is associated with relatively more transaction costs in addition to having to be carried out gradually over time, and for those reasons this is the most difficult change to make. This has implications for the endogeneity issues discussed below.

Advertising data were available for part of FY 2012 through ten months of FY 2018, thus defining the sample used to estimate the CPMs. Contract production models are econometrically estimated for all USAR NPS contracts and for USAR HQ contracts. USAR PS-CLG contracts are incorporated into the RRRM through user-supplied inputs.

This chapter discusses the submodels of the RRRM as depicted in Figure 4.1, including the USAR CPM and the cost allocation model.

The Contract Production Model

Following the approach in Knapp et al. (2018), our analysis is at the company level and takes recruiters as the key underlying resource necessary to create USAR contracts. Given the availability of advertising data, we use data from FY 2012 to FY 2018, during which team-based recruiting was the primary recruiting method used. Only companies with at least one positive USAR contract in each contract category (HQ and all NPS) are included in the analysis.

The Empirical Model

As in the RA CPM, we assume contracts are produced as a function of recruiters, mission, and qualified military individuals in the geography covered by a company in each month, with a shifting function that depends on the overall recruiting environment, the use of bonuses, and the level of television advertising. We also include controls for the calendar month and the number of days in a recruiting period for each month, as well as for one data outlier (the last month of 2015) in which contracts were considerably lower (statistically so) than in the rest of the data.

More formally, the USAR CPM takes the following form:

$$\ln \frac{C_{i,t}^q}{P_{i,t}} = \alpha_R \frac{R_{i,t}}{P_{i,t}} = \alpha_{USAR} \ln \frac{M_{i,t}^{USAR}}{P_{i,t}} + \alpha_{HQ} \ln \frac{M_{i,t}^{HQ}}{P_{i,t}} + \alpha_{RA} \ln \frac{M_{i,t}^{RA}}{P_{i,t}} +$$

$$f\left(RE_{i,t}, Bonus_{i,t}^q, Adstock_{i,t}, X_{i,t}, time_t\right) + \varepsilon_{it},$$

where

- $\frac{C_{i,t}^q}{P_{i,t}}$ is the number of contracts of type q (either all NPS contracts or HQ NPS contracts) for company i in recruiting contract month t, normalized by military-age population in the geographic area served by the company $P_{i,t}$[1]
- $\frac{R_{i,t}}{P_{i,t}}$ is the number of recruiters assigned to the company normalized by youth population
- $\frac{M_{i,t}^{USAR}}{P_{i,t}}$ is the total USAR recruiting mission for the company ($+1$ to account for potential zeros) normalized by youth population
- $\frac{M_{i,t}^{HQ}}{P_{i,t}}$ is the HQ USAR recruiting mission for the company ($+1$) normalized by youth population
- $\frac{M_{i,t}^{RA}}{P_{i,t}}$ is the RA recruiting mission for the company ($+1$) normalized by youth population
- the α's are coefficients to be estimated
- $f(\ )$ is the shifting function that depends on
  - $RE_{i,t}$, a vector of variables related to the recruiting environment including the unemployment rate, civilian-to-military wage ratio, Consumer Sentiment Index, and the minimum wage in a region for company i in month t
  - $Bonus_{i,t}^q$, which is a measure of expected MOS bonus spending; it is calculated as eligibility (operationalized as the share of contracts receiving an MOS bonus) multiplied by the average bonus amount conditional on receiving at least one bonus, multiplied by USAR recruiting mission for contract type q ($+1$ to account for potential zeros) for company i in month t

---

[1] Note that this normalization is also consistent with assuming constant returns to scale over recruiters, mission variables, and the military-aged population for a Cobb-Douglas production function.

- *Adstock$_{i,t}$*, which is a linear function of current and past advertising spending for company *i* in month *t*
- *X$_{i,t}$*, which is a vector of other controls, including month fixed effects, the number of days in a given recruiting contract month, the outlier indicator for FY 2015, month 12, and fixed company effects
- *time$_t$*, which is a fourth-degree polynomial in the time dimension
- $\varepsilon_{i,t}$ is a mean zero, constant variance error term.

This specification maintains the motivation in the RA CPM that recruiters, mission (as a proxy for effort), and population are the key inputs into contract production and that variables reflecting the recruiting environment, the use of bonuses and advertising, and other controls can shift the function on a month-to-month basis. The addition of the RA mission variable allows for substitution of effort between team recruiters as relative mission size changes for each component.

We investigated several variables expected to affect the recruiting environment, including the unemployment rate at the local level, the University of Michigan's Consumer Sentiment Index, the local civilian-to-military wage ratio, and the localized minimum wage rate. The hypothesized theoretical effect of these variables on USAR contracts is not as straightforward as it is for the RA, as civilian employment and military service are possibly complements in the USAR but substitutes for the RA. As such, an increase in, say, unemployment would not necessarily lead to an easier recruiting environment (and thus more contracts) for USAR. Unlike the model in Knapp et al. (2018), we chose to not include the (contracts minus mission)/contract mission for graduate alphas measure of recruiting difficulty from Wenger et al. (2019), since it was constructed as the (lagged average) difference between realized contracts (the dependent variable in the RA model) and mission for HQ high school graduate recruits, and is highly likely to be correlated with both the error term (creating an endogeneity problem) and the other measures of the recruiting environment (inducing multicollinearity).[2]

---

[2] We note that this research was done in parallel to a separate but related project updating the RA RRM, and the research teams worked together to make joint decisions on model specification in order to keep them parsimonious and similar in structure.

The $Adstock_{i,t}$ variable, and the way it enters into the USAR CPM, is somewhat different from the previously published RA CPM in Knapp et al. (2018), and offers a simplified linear-in-parameters approach that does not require nonlinear estimation methods. Following the work of Shapiro et al. (2020) and others, we define the "stock" of television advertising capital as $Adstock_{i,t} = \Sigma_{\tau=t-L}^{t}\delta^{t-\tau}a_{i,\tau}$, where $a_{i,t}$ is advertising spending assigned to company i in time t, $0<\delta<1$ is a weighting parameter, and L is a fixed number of lags.[3] As with the specification in Knapp et al. (2018) and Dertouzos and Garber (2003), this allows for carryover of television advertising spending, in that past spending can affect current behavior. Unlike the previous specification, however, we do not impose a symmetric functional form to obtain an S-shaped response; rather, we used and tested polynomials in $Adstock_{i,t}$ and ln $Adstock_{i,t}$ to see if the data reveal such a shape. While a cubic functional form in ln $Adstock_{i,t}$ has the disadvantage that the effect of advertising may not be monotonically increasing in the variable, we prefer to let the response curve be data driven rather than impose a given shape and believe that this model should be estimable for any data set that does not exhibit perfect collinearity.[4]

Finally, the fourth-degree polynomial in *time* provides a flexible way to control for all (unobserved) variables that vary only in the time dimension and affect each company in the same way, such as the national economic climate.

Model Structure and Endogeneity Issues

The USAR contract models are estimated using a company-level fixed-effects model. As with the RA CPM, estimation using data at the subnational level reduces the prospects of endogeneity in the policy variables (when the

---

[3] As in Knapp et al. (2018), we use the variation in dollars spent per impression within a company area to identify the returns to advertising. Furthermore, the effect of television advertising is assumed to be additive within the shifting function, meaning that it is substitutable with other variables in this function, but not directly with recruiters or contract mission.

[4] Attempts to estimate the USAR CPM and RA CPM with data for FY 2015–FY 2018 using the specification in Knapp et al. (2018) resulted in nonconvergence of the nonlinear algorithm.

outcome of interest influences the use of certain policy levers), since these decisions are often outside the local commander's control.

Nevertheless, endogeneity can still be a problem, especially if all companies are experiencing a common shock (hence the inclusion of the polynomial time terms to help control for the impacts of all time-varying-only variables). Endogenous relationships can result in seemingly counterintuitive results, such as a negative sign on variables related to bonuses because bonus eligibility or levels are increased in times when recruiting (and thus generating contracts) is difficult. Ideally, the coefficient estimates in the CPMs reflect the *structural*, or causal, parameters of the production function (equivalently, the effect without the endogenous confounding). In this case, it is bonus-related variables that are likely to be the most affected, since the Army can, budget permitting, rapidly deploy them in times of a negative shock to contract production; however, television advertising spending and recruiters may also change in response to negative shocks, albeit more slowly.

The problem of endogeneity is typically solved using *instruments*, variables that are correlated with the endogenous regressor but not correlated with the error term. We were unable to identify suitable instruments for the policy variables and view the inclusion of the time controls and estimation at the company level as the best solution available. Nevertheless, readers should understand that endogeneity of the explanatory variables could result in parameter estimates that are biased and inconsistent.

A Summary of the Data and Estimation of U.S. Army Reserve Contract Production

Table 4.1 presents the summary statistics of the data used to estimate the all-contracts CPM, including all NPS contracts for USAR for FY 2012–FY 2018.[5] The average company produced just under five contracts per recruiting contract month over this period from an average potential population size of just under 41,000 young people. We note that this is, on average, less than

---

[5] Television advertising data are available starting in FY 2012, while other variables are generally available from August 2002 through FY 2018. However, as television advertising spending is a key policy variable, we restrict attention to the period for which all data are available. PS-CLG contracts are not used in CPM estimation, as they are a direct input into the RRRM.

TABLE 4.1

Descriptive Statistics for Recruiting Companies Used in the Reserve Contract Production Model

Variable	Mean	Standard Deviation	Minimum	Maximum
USAR HQ contracts	4.7	3.1	1.0	38.0
Youth population	40,863.1	14,912.6	2,310.0	119,202.0
Recruiters	31.7	9.0	6.0	68.0
USAR total mission	6.3	3.3	0.0	54.0
USAR HQ mission	3.7	2.1	0.0	39.0
RA mission	25.5	10.1	0.0	86.0
Consumer sentiment	122.7	11.0	97.63	141.6
Unemployment rate	6.0	2.0	2.0	17.6
Civilian-to-military wage ratio	0.9	0.1	0.6	1.3
Minimum wage (dollars per hour)	8.00	1.00	7.30	13.30
Expected MOS bonus spending (dollars per company)	24,358.20	29,788.50	0.00	369,600.00
Television advertising spending (in thousands of dollars)	14.4	18.6	0.0	224.5
Days in RCM	20.3	3.0	8.0	32.0

NOTES: Data at the company RCM level are for all companies with nonzero contracts for FY 2012–FY 2018 (the time period for which all variables are generally available). USAR HQ contracts are all NPS contracts. Minimum and maximum days in RCM reflect changes in the way the Army defined contract months in FY 2014–FY 2015, with the eight-day month dropped from the estimation (September 2015). Sample size for each variable = 17,151.

the mission size of 6.3 contracts; the company-level recruiting goals for the USAR for mostly NPS contracts were about 25 percent of those for the RA (recall that recruitment for both components is done by the same recruiting unit). Television prospect advertising spending averaged $14,400 per company, with some significant variation over space and time, which aggregates to between $14 million and $64 million per year. We note that this is considerably less than current advertising expenditures. Expected bonus spending was about $24,400 per month, corresponding to overall eligibility rates that ranged from about 20 percent to about 80 percent depending on the company and time period. Bonus eligibility rates changed rapidly in the data over time, as shown in Chapter Two, suggesting that enlistment bonuses were used as an immediate policy lever to try to meet the accession mission.

While the economic environment during this time period varied across companies and time, there is generally a monotonic relationship between time and unemployment for each company in the data. The data essentially begin immediately after the Great Recession (around 2008–2011), and the population-weighted unemployment time series exhibits a strong downward trend from the start of the data through the end of the series.[6] Consumer sentiment is negatively correlated with unemployment, and thus is increasing over most of this time period.[7]

To implement the USAR CPM, monthly advertising spending needs to be put into its capital stock form ($Adstock_{i,t}$). As in Shapiro et al. (2020), we used a grid search procedure to test various values (δ) ranging from 0.1 to 0.9 and lag lengths (L) from zero to 9. Criteria for evaluation included R-squared, root mean squared error, and correlation between predicted and actual contract levels. We found that the optimal empirical specification that maximized predictive power and minimized root mean squared error was a lag of 1 and a δ weight of 0.1. While using fewer lags and less weight on those lags than the model in Knapp et al. (2018), this specification is driven by the data and allows for the retention of observations at the beginning of the series.

Results of the fixed-effects estimation are shown in Table 4.2, in which we present the unrestricted model and the final specification used for the excursions in Chapter Five.[8]

---

[6] Weighting by youth population in the region served by each company provides a way to examine a single time series in unemployment in a manner consistent with the data used to estimate the CPM.

[7] Running a fixed effects regression of consumer sentiment in the data against a cubic polynomial in unemployment and graphing the results shows that the series are almost indistinguishable save for very low levels of unemployment—when the Consumer Sentiment Index flattens. Results are available from the authors.

[8] Although we choose to use the restricted model for the results that follow in Chapter Five due to the lower variance of the estimates, assuming the restrictions are true and for parsimony, we note that restrictions on television advertising spending and environmental variables shift the contract production function in a technologically neutral manner. As such, using the full specification may change the total estimated costs reported in Chapter Five, but qualitative conclusions about relative recruiting resource use are unlikely to change.

TABLE 4.2

The Contract Production Model for All U.S. Army Reserve Non–Prior Service Contracts

Variable	Model 1 (Full Specification)	Model 2 (Restricted, Final Specification)
ln (recruiters/youth population)	0.431***	0.426***
	(0.0400)	(0.0399)
ln ([USAR total mission + 1]/youth population)	0.331***	0.330***
	(0.0230)	(0.0230)
ln ([USAR HQ mission + 1]/youth population)	0.121***	0.122***
	(0.0200)	(0.0200)
ln ([RA mission + 1]/youth population)	−0.205***	−0.204***
	(0.0196)	(0.0195)
ln (unemployment rate)	−0.0345	—
	(0.0421)	
ln (civilian-to-military wage ratio)	0.288	—
	(0.174)	
ln (Consumer Sentiment Index)	0.0536	—
	(0.107)	
ln (minimum wage)	−0.470***	−0.478***
	(0.0792)	(0.0782)
ln (expected MOS bonus spending + 1)	0.0409***	0.0410***
	(0.00106)	(0.00106)
ln (*Adstock*)	0.0400	0.0303***
	(0.0272)	(0.00602)
ln (*Adstock*)_squared	−0.0118	—
	(0.0127)	

Table 4.2—Continued

Variable	Model 1 (Full Specification)	Model 2 (Restricted, Final Specification)
In (*Adstock*)_cubed	0.00226	—
	(0.00182)	
Days in RCM	0.0264***	0.0263***
	(0.00169)	(0.00168)
Outlier	−0.434***	−0.437***
	(0.0582)	(0.0581)
October (omitted)		
November	−0.0560**	−0.0570**
	(0.0213)	(0.0212)
December	0.0809***	0.0812***
	(0.0204)	(0.0203)
January	−0.0548*	−0.0509*
	(0.0214)	(0.0211)
February	0.0942***	0.0909***
	(0.0211)	(0.0200)
March	0.0157	0.0121
	(0.0211)	(0.0202)
April	0.0883***	0.0878***
	(0.0205)	(0.0201)
May	−0.0834***	−0.0810***
	(0.0207)	(0.0202)
June	−0.0963***	−0.0942***
	(0.0206)	(0.0204)

Table 4.2—Continued

Variable	Model 1 (Full Specification)	Model 2 (Restricted, Final Specification)
July	−0.117***	−0.121***
	(0.0209)	(0.0205)
August	−0.159***	−0.162***
	(0.0215)	(0.0211)
September	−0.138***	−0.140***
	(0.0226)	(0.0224)
Time	2.781***	2.745***
	(0.329)	(0.318)
Time_squared	−0.0290***	−0.0287***
	(0.00329)	(0.00318)
Time_cubed	0.000133***	0.000132***
	(0.0000145)	(0.0000140)
Time_fourth	−0.000000228***	−0.000000227***
	(2.36e − 08)	(2.28e − 08)
Constant	−103.2***	−101.4***
	(12.25)	(11.84)
Observations	17,151	17,151
Within R^2	0.2541	0.2539
Between R^2	0.7384	0.7607
Overall R^2	0.3649	0.3697

NOTES: Standard errors in parentheses. $^*p < 0.05$, $^{**}p < 0.01$, $^{***}p < 0.001$. There were 248 unique company identifiers (fixed effects), with an average of 69.2 observations per group (minimum 1, maximum 80). Dependent variable is ln ([NPS contracts]/youth population). Data are from FY 2012–FY 2018.

We first note that the primary variables of interest (inputs into production, policy variables, and environment variables) enter the model in log form and can be interpreted (for variables entering linearly) as elasticities. For example, for Model 1, the coefficient of 0.431 on recruiters normalized by population is interpreted as a 10-percent increase in recruiters, as companies will, on average, increase contract production by 4.3 percent, all else equal.[9] The positive sign matches theory, as we expect that more recruiters would result in more recruiting effort and thus more USAR contracts.

Turning to the mission variables, we find positive signs and plausible elasticity magnitudes on the coefficients for total mission and HQ mission, suggesting that increasing mission, all else equal, can change the behavior of recruiters and tends to result in a greater number of contracts. However, the negative sign on RA mission suggests that effort between the USAR and RA are substitutes rather than complements. In other words, if the RA mission increases without any other changes, recruiters face an incentive to shift effort toward recruiting RA soldiers at the expense of USAR contracts. Given the team recruiting concept, it would not be prudent to ignore the RA mission when predicting USAR accessions.

Notably, we find that three of the four environmental variables are statistically insignificant in the unrestricted specification (Model 1). As noted in Chapter One, the effect of the recruiting environment on RA and USAR recruiting may differ, and there appears to be statistical evidence to support this proposition. There are several possible explanations for this result. First, from a statistical standpoint, it could be that the correlation between unemployment, the Consumer Sentiment Index, and the civilian-to-military wage ratio is causing inflated standard errors on these variables (the former two variables, in particular, move very closely together). Another behavioral explanation might be that USAR enlistment is driven more by (unobservable) "propensity to serve" considerations than economic considerations. That is, unlike in the RA, civilian employment is a complement to USAR service rather than a substitute for it. The positive signs on the civilian-to-military wage ratio and consumer sentiment variables, coupled with the negative sign on the unemployment variable, support this hypothesis.

---

[9] Note that diminishing marginal returns is implied by this result.

However, the sign on the minimum wage variable is negative (and significant), suggesting that as the minimum wage goes up, potential enlistees are less likely to join USAR (a substitute relationship that mirrors the substitute relationship found in Knapp et al., 2018). Although we cannot definitively answer why these variables are insignificant, imposing zero coefficient restrictions on them (i.e., dropping them from the model) does little to affect explanatory power, and the other coefficients appear quite stable.[10]

Indeed, the positive and significant sign on the bonus variable suggests that financial incentives *can* have a positive effect on USAR accessions (elasticity = .04), meaning that, on average, recruits are not *solely* motivated by nonpecuniary preferences. The elasticity of 0.04 implies that a 10-percent increase in bonus spending results in a 0.4-percent increase in expected contracts. However, given the remaining potential endogeneity problems associated with bonus use, it seems likely that this may be an underestimate of the efficacy of bonuses, as their use is likely positively correlated with (unobservable) negative shocks to contract production.[11]

Finally, turning to the television advertising stock variable, we first allowed it to enter in a cubic formulation, which allows for, but does not impose, an S-shaped response of contracts to advertising (and lagged advertising) spending. Using the point estimates from the cubic specification in Model 1, we find some evidence of an S-shaped response for low levels of advertising, as overall elasticity estimates are negative (recall that a cubic function does not impose monotonicity), followed by a period of positive

---

[10] Although it does not control for other variables or variation across space, graphing population-weighted unemployment rates against total USAR contracts from FY 2012–FY 2018 shows that the unemployment rate is clearly dropping over the time period, while contracts remain relatively constant. The lack of a sustained period where the unemployment rate tends to rise in this data could also be a contributing factor to the result.

[11] While we focus the discussion on the possible downward bias of the bonus variables, it should be noted that the other policy levers may also suffer from endogeneity issues, though the relatively larger transactions costs associated with their use by the Army in times of production shocks should mitigate this problem somewhat. We further note then when testing various model specifications, coefficients on television advertising spending and recruiters were universally positive and generally stable in magnitude, while the coefficient on bonus use was negative when the polynomial time trend was excluded.

but diminishing marginal returns (as would be expected). However, at larger levels of advertising spending, the elasticity curve begins to increase at a greater rate, in defiance of theory and expectations. The most likely explanation from a statistical perspective is that there are a few relatively large outliers in the data, and these outliers are driving the shape of the response curve. Indeed, when we only include *ln Adstock* in Model 2, the elasticity with respect to the stock variable is a reasonable 0.03, suggesting that a 10-percent change in the advertising stock is associated with a 0.3-percent change in contracts. This estimate is in line with the results presented in Shapiro et al. (2020) for consumer goods advertising, as well as other estimates in the more recent literature. As with the environment variables, the other coefficient estimates are stable when imposing zero restrictions on the squared and cubic terms, and the positive and significant coefficient on the linear term suggests diminishing marginal returns to advertising spending. We thus use Model 2 for our final specification.

A Summary of the Data and Estimation of High Quality U.S. Army Reserve Contract Production

Following Knapp et al. (2018), we allow the CPM for HQ recruits (high school graduate alphas and high school senior alphas) to differ from that of all contracts. Theoretically, these recruits have a different opportunity set than do potential non-HQ enlistees, which could manifest itself in different contract production relationships.[12] As in the RA RRM, we define predicted non-HQ contracts as the difference between the all-contracts USAR CPM and the USAR HQ CPM, with realized non-HQ contracts dependent on USAR's willingness to accept non-HQ contracts based on operational considerations. We discuss this in more detail in Chapter Five.

The summary statistics for the variables used for the USAR HQ CPM are reported in Table 4.3. Most of the variables used in the HQ model are identical to the previous model, save for the dependent variable (HQ contracts) and the expected bonus variable, which is calculated from the HQ data only. The summary statistics and sample size differ, as not all companies with positive contracts in an RCM also have positive HQ contracts. As

---

[12] All USAR HQ contracts in the data are NPS contracts.

TABLE 4.3

Descriptive Statistics for Recruiting Companies Used in the High Quality Reserve Contract Production Model

	Mean	Standard Deviation	Minimum	Maximum
USAR HQ contracts	2.9	2.0	1.0	24.0
Youth population	41,374.0	15,024.1	2310.0	119,202.0
Recruiters	31.9	9.0	6.0	68.0
USAR total mission	6.5	3.3	0.0	54.0
USAR HQ mission	3.8	2.1	0.0	39.0
RA mission	25.6	10.2	0.0	86.0
Consumer sentiment	122.7	12.0	97.63	141.6
Unemployment rate	6.0	1.9	2.0	17.6
Civilian-to-military wage ratio	0.9	0.1	0.6	1.3
Minimum wage (dollars per hour)	8.00	1.00	7.30	13.30
Expected HQ MOS bonus spending (dollars per company)	11,738.20	16,228.90	0.00	173,250.00
Television advertising spending (in thousands of dollars)	14.7	19.0	0.0	224.5
Days in RCM	20.4	3.0	8.0	32.0

NOTES: Data are at the company RCM level for all companies with nonzero contracts for FY 2012–FY 2018 (the time period for which all variables are generally available). USAR HQ contracts are all NPS HQ contracts. Minimum and maximum days in RCM reflect changes in the way the Army defined contract months in FY 2014–FY 2015, with the eight-day month dropped from the estimation (September 2015). Sample size for each variable = 15,472.

seen by comparing contract numbers from Tables 4.1 and 4.3, the average company recruits about 60 percent (three out of five) HQ recruits. Bonus eligibility (a component of expected bonus spending) for HQ recruits is about 62 percent on average, compared with 32 percent for non-HQ contracts. Average bonus amounts for HQ recruits, conditional on receiving a bonus, were just over $9,500; the corresponding figure for non-HQ contracts was about $6,650.

Results of the fixed-effects estimation for the USAR HQ CPM are presented in Table 4.4.

TABLE 4.4

The Contract Production Model for High Quality Non–Prior Service Contracts

Variable	Model 1 (Full Specification)	Model 2 (Restricted, Final Specification)
ln ([recruiters]/youth population)	0.430***	0.424***
	(0.0430)	(0.0429)
ln ([USAR total mission + 1]/youth population)	0.246***	0.267***
	(0.0250)	(0.0142)
ln ([USAR HQ mission + 1]/youth population)	0.0229	—
	(0.0219)	
ln ([RA mission + 1]/youth population)	−0.136***	−0.137***
	(0.0211)	(0.0210)
ln (unemployment rate)	−0.0388	—
	(0.0454)	
ln (civilian-to-military wage ratio)	0.488**	—
	(0.186)	
ln (Consumer Sentiment Index)	−0.199	—
	(0.114)	
ln (minimum wage)	−0.231**	−0.247**
	(0.0847)	(0.0836)
ln (expected HQ MOS bonus spending + 1)	0.0404***	0.0405***
	(0.00103)	(0.00102)
ln (Adstock)	−0.0207	0.0288***
	(0.0291)	(0.00643)
ln (Adstock)_squared	0.0130	—
	(0.0135)	
ln (Adstock)_cubed	−0.000548	—
	(0.00193)	

Table 4.4—Continued

Variable	Model 1 (Full Specification)	Model 2 (Restricted, Final Specification)
Days in RCM	0.0206***	0.0200***
	(0.00180)	(0.00179)
Outlier	−0.317***	−0.324***
	(0.0680)	(0.0678)
October (omitted)		
November	−0.0365	−0.0430
	(0.0227)	(0.0226)
December	0.0418	0.0367
	(0.0217)	(0.0215)
January	−0.0309	−0.0323
	(0.0228)	(0.0225)
February	0.0611**	0.0453*
	(0.0224)	(0.0212)
March	0.0156	0.000205
	(0.0226)	(0.0216)
April	0.0818***	0.0711***
	(0.0218)	(0.0213)
May	0.0123	0.000960
	(0.0221)	(0.0216)
June	−0.0277	−0.0338
	(0.0219)	(0.0217)
July	−0.0511*	−0.0623**
	(0.0223)	(0.0219)
August	−0.0420	−0.0517*
	(0.0229)	(0.0224)

Table 4.4—Continued

Variable	Model 1 (Full Specification)	Model 2 (Restricted, Final Specification)
September	−0.0632**	−0.0690**
	(0.0242)	(0.0240)
Time	1.579***	1.674***
	(0.352)	(0.341)
Time_squared	−0.0169***	−0.0180***
	(0.00351)	(0.00340)
Time_cubed	0.0000800***	0.0000850***
	(0.0000155)	(0.0000149)
Time_fourth	−0.000000141***	−0.000000149***
	(2.53e − 08)	(2.44e − 08)
Constant	−59.21***	−63.37***
	(13.11)	(12.68)
Observations	15,472	15,472
Within R^2	0.1866	0.1856
Between R^2	0.5990	0.6521
Overall R^2	0.2637	0.2718

NOTES: Standard errors in parentheses. $*p < 0.05$, $**p < 0.01$, $***p < 0.001$. There were 248 unique company identifiers (fixed effects) with an average of 62.4 observations per group (minimum 1, maximum 80). Dependent variable is ln ([HQ NPS contracts]/youth population). Data are from FY 2012–FY 2018.

As with the all-contracts model, the signs on the coefficients for the USAR HQ CPM align with what theory would predict, with recruiters and USAR mission exhibiting positive elasticities. In addition, as in the previous model, an increase in RA mission causes a decline in USAR HQ contracts. While the magnitude of the response of HQ contracts to recruiters is similar to the previous model, the responsiveness to the other mission variables is lower, and the HQ mission variable is not significantly different from zero. It is not completely clear why this is the case in the HQ model and not the all-contracts model; however, we note that a positive relationship is maintained for overall USAR mission and that historically, achieving the total mission has taken precedence over meeting the HQ goal in difficult recruiting periods.

Unlike the previous model, the ratio of median high school male civilian earnings to military compensation is positive and significant in Model 1, which implies that USAR contracts increase as median high school male earnings increase. This is a counterintuitive result, and in testing various model specifications, we found the coefficient to be relatively unstable. One possible explanation would be the presence of collinearity between the environment variables. Another is that an increasing civilian wage increases the attractiveness of USAR service relative to full-time military service.[13] Due to this parameter's instability, however, we ultimately chose to exclude this variable from the final specification, though we acknowledge that future research should retest this relationship, especially if new data include a deteriorating economic environment.[14] Of the other environment variables, only the local minimum wage was statistically significant, with a negative sign but lower magnitude than in the all-contracts model.

The effect of expected bonus spending in the USAR HQ CPM is essentially the same as the all-contracts model, with a 10-percent change in bonus spending resulting in about a 0.4-percent increase in HQ contracts. Finally, the response to advertising is positive and about the same size for HQ recruits as for all recruits, with an estimated elasticity just below 0.03.[15]

Operationalizing the Contract Production Models in the Reserve Recruiting Resource Model

In the RRRM, the CPM maps the resources available to all contracts and HQ contracts, with the marginal product of the resource, in part, determining the marginal costs associated with a USAR accession. Unlike the RA RRM, there is no DEP model for the RRRM, as contract signers are

---

[13] We thank our reviewer for this possible interpretation.

[14] We note that excluding the civilian-to-military wage ratio actually improves predictive power of the model over a specification that includes it.

[15] Readers are reminded that the model focused on HQ recruits may suffer the same endogeneity problems as the all-contracts model.

assumed to report directly to their units. However, as with the RA RRM, a cost allocation model completes the full model. Accessions and recruit quality remain the two main goals of the recruiting enterprise, and the RRRM is designed to help planners minimize the cost of accomplishing these goals.

To operationalize the USAR CPM, we largely follow the methods documented in Knapp et al. (2018). In particular, in order to avoid the need to specify company-level resources, we apportion user-supplied resource assumptions (including missioning for USAR contracts, USAR HQ contract share, RA mission, initial recruiters, and television advertising dollars) in accordance with their shares in FY 2017 (the last full year for which we have full data). Contracting days and the minimum wage in each RCM are assumed to be the same as in FY 2017. PS contracts are specified by the user and assumed to be non-HQ for the purposes of the model.[16] Users also specify the initial bonus eligibility percentage for all contracts and HQ contracts, as well as the initial average dollar amount of such a bonus, though the RRRM optimizes over these variables.

Following specification and allocation of the inputs to the USAR CPM (i.e., the explanatory variables of Model 2), the equations produce estimates of monthly NPS contracts and HQ contracts and are added to the PS-CLG contracts specified by the user. We maintain the assumption from Knapp et al. (2018) that any "excess" non-HQ contracts are not signed, reflecting selectivity on behalf of USAR with respect to quality.

Waivers are treated similarly to the RA RRM in that the number of contracts (both non-HQ and HQ) are proportionally adjusted from the rate in the data (about 8 percent) using the formula

$$C_{post} = C_{pre} \times \left(\frac{0.92}{1} - w_{target} \right),$$

where C_{post} is the number of contracts (all or HQ) after the adjustment, C_{pre} is the number of contracts estimated by the USAR CPM, 0.92 is 1 minus the historical waiver rate, and w_{target} is the target rate of waivers specified by the user. As such, an increase in the target waiver rate will cause the multiplier (in parentheses in the formula) to be greater than 1, and the estimated number of contracts will increase.

---

[16] The HQ percentages reported in this chapter refer only to NPS contracts.

The USAR CPM thus takes the following values as inputs: resourcing levels, eligibility policy (such as waiver rates, the HQ mission, and the number of PS contracts), and the assumed distribution of companies, recruiters, minimum wage, and advertising spending from a reference period or by user design. We note that this version of the RRRM excludes the three excluded recruiting environment variables (unemployment rate, civilian-to-military wage ratio, and Consumer Sentiment Index), but future iterations may include these or similar measures. The outputs of the CPM are the number of contracts by type (HQ contracts or all NPS contracts).

The Cost Allocation Model

Several assumptions are needed to complete the RRRM costing procedure. First, recruiter annual costs are assumed to be $111,324 per year, or just under $9,300 per month.[17] Total recruiter costs are the number of on-production recruiters operating in a recruiting contract month times this value. Bonus costs are assumed to be the product of the contracts assumed to receive a bonus (by type) multiplied by the relevant average bonus amount. The optimization model directly solves for television prospect advertising spending.

The USAR cost allocation model takes these assumptions and the outputs of the USAR CPM as inputs, and outputs total resourcing costs by month by resource type.

Innovations in the Reserve Recruiting Resource Model

As documented herein, we made several simplifications to the specification in Knapp et al. (2018) in order to speed estimation and more accurately reflect the relationships between the explanatory variables and USAR contract production. In particular, we changed the specification for how television advertising entered the model, using a linear-in-parameters functional form, and used a cubic polynomial to retain the possibility of an S-shaped

---

[17] This value was provided to the RAND Arroyo Center by the HQDA.

response of contracts to advertising. This allows for a nonlinear response and to use standard, linear fixed-effects estimation instead of a nonlinear maximum likelihood solver.

We also incorporated the RA accession mission into the specification to model the potential substitution of effort toward RA enlistees if the mission is increased. We represent MOS bonuses as an "expectation" on bonus spending calculated by multiplying eligibility percentages by average bonus level for all contracts and HQ contracts and then multiplying this average by USAR mission. This eliminates the need to construct a separate factor model for bonuses, as was done for the RA RRM, and eases interpretation of the resultant coefficients. This also allows for optimization over bonus amounts, reflecting changes in eligibility and average bonus amounts conditional on receiving one.

Finally, to (at least partially) control for the potential endogeneity of the policy levers and any other variables that may affect all recruiting companies in the same manner over time, we incorporate a polynomial of order four in time.

CHAPTER FIVE

Model Demonstration and Optimization

The RRRM is used to predict how a chosen set of recruiting resources and recruit eligibility policies combine to produce USAR accessions and the cost of doing so. With this information, planners can determine the sufficiency of resource plans to meet accession and quality objectives for USAR or explore how to optimize resource plans to minimize costs conditional on meeting those goals. We note that, as of the time of writing this report, the RRRM is optimizing only over USAR missioning and quality objectives and using the CPM estimated for USAR only. In addition, the RA CPM is different (for example, in that model, the unemployment rate is a key variable reflecting the effect of the recruiting environment). As such, the results presented in this chapter should be interpreted as informative regarding resourcing levels needed to meet only USAR accession goals. It is *not* the case that the optimal resource mix found in the results of this chapter are optimal for the RA or the joint objectives of both components. It would be desirable to link the models with a joint objective function in future work in order to optimize resource distributions subject to accession goals for both the RA and USAR.

This chapter describes the objective function used in the RRRM optimization routine and presents the results of several excursions to illustrate the utility of the tool for USAR. Starting from a set of assumed baseline resourcing, environment, and eligibility policies, we investigate changes in

- accession goals for both USAR and RA
- resourcing strategies with different missioning levels
- eligibility policy (the use of waivers and the target HQ percentage).

We also test the implications of combining changes in accession goals and eligibility policy on feasibility and recruiting costs.

The Reserve Recruiting Resource Model Optimization Objective Function

The objective of the RRRM is to estimate the cost-minimizing set of recruiting inputs subject to overall accession goals (based on USAR unit vacancies), quality objectives (the target HQ rate), percentage of waiver contracts, number of PS accessions, recruiting environment (in this model, the minimum wage), and initial resource levels (e.g., recruiters and prior television advertising spending). The RRRM does not include a DEP, so there are no DEP-related goals or initial values.

In formulating the cost minimization routine, we considered the real-world constraints on Army resource use and variability, as well as the facts that the Army is very motivated to "make mission" each year but willing to trade off monthly overages and deficiencies between months. As such, the objective function includes not only the cost of optimized resource use but also terms that represent preferences with respect to monthly deviations from mission and from overall annual mission. In addition, given the transaction costs associated with changing recruiter numbers, we add a hard constraint that limits changes to recruiter numbers on a month-to-month basis.

To be consistent with the RA RRM, this problem is implemented as an unconstrained optimization problem based on a weighted objective function that represents trade-offs between accession goals and costs.[1] These subobjectives are combined using weights on current accession goals that represent USAR's "willingness to pay" to avoid not meeting the target. A higher weight indicates a greater willingness to pay to avoid missing the subobjective, and thus implicitly determines when the optimization algorithm stops allocating resources to achieve the nonmonetary mission goals,

---

[1] This was termed the "criterion value" in Knapp et al. (2018).

ostensibly because doing so is "too expensive." This specification implicitly imposes the HQ percentage goals for whatever level of accessions results from the optimization.[2]

The objective function in the RRRM is defined as follows. Let $AOdiff_t$ be the difference between the overall USAR mission (NPS and PS-CLG contracts) and the realized contracts in recruiting contract month t, conditional on the resources currently assigned (with shortfalls denoted as negative); $Cost_t$ is the obligated costs of those resources for time t. The objective function for a given fiscal year is defined as

$$Obj = \Sigma_{t=1}^{12} f(AOdiff_t, w_{A0}) + Cost_t + I(Annual\ Mission > Annual\ Contract) \times 10^{20},$$

where

$$f(AOdiff_t, w_{A0}) = \begin{cases} w_{A0,1} = AOdiff_t^2 \text{ if } AOdiff_t < 0 \\ w_{A0,2} = AOdiff_t^2 \text{ if } AOdiff_t \geq 0 \end{cases}$$

$I(\ )$ is a binary indicator that equals 1 if annual contracts are less than annual mission, and $w_{A0,j}$ are scalar weighting parameters that penalize any differential between target and realized accessions in month t. The chosen weights, based on in-sample testing of the RA RRM, are $w_{A0,1} = 1,500$ and $w_{A0,2} = 750$.[3] There are several things to note about this specification. First, the binary indicator function is new to the RRRM, and places a considerable penalty (10^{20}) on missing the overall yearly mission. This prioritizes meeting annual mission if it is at all feasible, forcing the optimization algorithm to restrict attention to the region where total mission is met. In other words, it functions as a hard constraint on meeting annual mission. Second, the monthly weights are much smaller but smoothly depend on the difference between contracts and mission in a given month, implying that a shortfall of

---

[2] Future iterations of the RA RRM and RRRM could explicitly include quality differentials as an additional subobjective; that would require the choice of weights to represent the trade-offs between total accessions and quality targets.

[3] The positive weight on exceeding monthly mission ensures that the algorithm does return a contract distribution over months that significantly deviates from assumed monthly missioning targets.

X contracts is worth $\$1,500 \times X^2$ to avoid. For example, a 100-unit vacancy shortfall is equivalent to $\$15$ million. Note that the cost increases as the differential between accession targets and realized contracts increases, which means that month-to-month shortfalls are penalized more as the monthly mission deficit increases.[4]

An optimal solution is attained by minimizing the 12-month objective function specified above, subject to constraints. The optimizer simultaneously searches over the entire 72-dimensional parameter space—defined by monthly recruiter values, advertising amounts, HQ bonus levels, HQ eligibility levels, average bonus levels, and average eligibility levels—to derive an optimal solution. We use the Constrained Optimization by Linear Approximation (COBYLA) algorithm to perform this optimization (Powell, 1994). The COBYLA algorithm operates by first generating a linear approximation of the objective function, centered around the initialization. This linear approximation is then optimized over a trust region in the space of parameters. This process continues, decreasing the volume of the trust region in each iteration, until convergence. The COBYLA algorithm is a local optimization algorithm. While solutions improve upon the initialized parameters, they are not guaranteed to converge on a globally optimal solution.

Like the RA RRM, there are several additional constraints and assumptions imposed on the RRRM to reflect real-world conditions:

- The number of recruiters cannot increase by more than 1.6 percent from month to month and cannot decrease by more than 1.0 percent per month (with these numbers derived from the data used in Knapp et al., 2018) in order to reflect workforce realities. However, this constraint is not applied to the difference in the initial recruiting numbers and the first period of contract production.
- Bonus incentives are limited to $\$20,000$ and 80 percent for all contracts and $\$20,000$ and 90 percent for HQ contracts, which is consistent with the range seen in the data.

---

[4] As a tool suitable for strategic planning purposes, uncertainty over recruiting outcomes is not explicitly modeled.

- PS-CLG contracts are entered as an input by the user. For the excursions presented below, we assume 800 PS contracts for excursions with a USAR mission of 15,000, and 1,333 for those with a USAR mission of 25,000 (5.33 percent), roughly equal to the share of PS contracts as a percentage of mission in FY 2017 (the last year for which we have complete data).
- HQ eligibility and bonus levels cannot be lower than overall average eligibility and bonus levels.

While the CPM is specified at the company level, several key parameters are defined at an aggregate level (i.e., summed across all companies in each month). These parameters include the RA mission, the USAR mission, advertising spending, and the number of recruiters. For each of these variables we allocate company-specific values according to their share of the total measured in FY 2017. For example, if R_t refers to the total number of recruiters in month t, then the number of recruiters assigned to company i in month t will be

$$R_{i,t} = R_t \frac{R_{i,t}^{2017}}{\Sigma_i R_{i,t}^{2017}}$$

where $R_{i,t}^{2017}$ refers to the number of recruiters in company i in month t in 2017. Analogous proportional allocation occurs for the mission and advertising spending variables. Note that USAR and RA missions are defined once before optimization, varying across excursion. However, recruiter and advertising spending are both optimized. Consequently, this proportionate allocation occurs once at every iteration of the optimization.

The optimized results from the RRRM are either a cost-minimized allocation of resources that meets USAR accession and quality targets or the allocation of resources that minimizes the objective function and produces as many contracts as possible. Accession goals are entered by the user on a monthly basis, and thus describe a USAR unit vacancy fill distribution over the course of a year. In the following sections we provide the results of several excursions designed by the research team to illustrate the use of the RRRM in practice.

Baseline Resourcing and Eligibility Assumptions

Based roughly on recent history and recruiting plans for USAR, the research team developed the following baseline recruiting resource and recruit eligibility plan:[5]

- Resources:
  - MOS bonuses: 50-percent bonus eligibility for HQ contracts, with an $8,000 average bonus conditional on receiving one; 35-percent bonus eligibility overall, with an overall average bonus of $7,850. This corresponds to levels near the means of the data.
  - Television prospect advertising: $10.9 million per month, including the month prior to the fiscal year. This corresponds roughly to recent television prospect advertising.[6]
  - Recruiters: 9,000 on-production recruiters per month. This corresponds roughly to recent team recruiter levels.
- Recruit eligibility:
  - HQ percentage: 67.9 percent with traditional high school diplomas and scoring in the top half of the AFQT score distribution. This corresponds to the HQ percentage in the data.
  - Enlistment waivers: 10 percent with waivers. This is slightly higher than the 8-percent average in the data used to estimate the model.
  - PS-CLG accessions: Set to equal 800, which is roughly equivalent to the number of PS accessions in FY 2017.[7]
- Recruiting environment:
  - Minimum wage: Average of baseline year of FY 2017 in company's recruiting area.

---

[5] The research team developed the baseline assumptions in conjunction with the sponsor to reflect a baseline (and meaningful excursions from it) for planning and informational purposes relevant to USAR.

[6] This level of television prospect advertising, while tied to recent levels, is out of sample for the data used to construct the RRRM. Peak annual advertising spending was observed in FY 2016, at about $65 million. We assume that the elasticity of approximately .03 holds at the larger resource level.

[7] In cases where a representative year was needed to develop baseline assumptions, we used FY 2017 as the last complete year for which we had data.

- Missioning:
  - USAR NPS and PS-CLG accession missions: 15,000.
  - RA accession mission: 69,000.

Without optimizing, the RRRM predicts that this combination of resources, eligibility policies, and environment would result in 16,167 USAR accessions in the fiscal year for which these assumptions hold. The total cost is estimated at $1.177 billion, divided 85 percent, 11 percent, and 4 percent among recruiters ($1.002 billion), television prospect advertising ($131 million), and MOS bonus incentives ($44 million), respectively.[8] Average contract production per month is 1,347. These results indicate that this resourcing plan would be more than sufficient to meet the original fiscal year baseline 2018 objective of 15,000 accessions, 95 percent of which are NPS contracts.

This overproduction of contracts implies that the USAR contract mission can be met for a lower total cost, and it is possible that a reallocation among resource categories can further improve efficiency. To test this hypothesis, we turn to the optimization algorithm, which is used to minimize the objective function by changing the number of recruiters (subject to the monthly change constraints), television prospect advertising, and the use of MOS bonuses. Beginning with the baseline parameters and solving, the RRRM finds a solution with the total number of contracts equal to the total mission. In addition, we find the following, as seen in Table 5.1:

- Minimum resource requirements for a 15,000-accession mission are $1.006 billion, a 14.5-percent decrease from the baseline parameterization.
- The resource savings from not recruiting the 1,167 "extra" USAR soldiers at the nonoptimized cost per recruit is about $85 million. Since the total cost savings from optimizing is bigger than this amount, there are savings from changing the distribution of spending across resources.
- Both the levels and distribution of recruiting spending changed:
  - All categories of recruiting resource spending declined.

---

[8] Recruiter costs supplied by HQDA is based on compensation and other factors rather than recruiting operations. Television prospect advertising cost represents the cost of media buys and, thus, is a subset of all marketing costs.

TABLE 5.1

Optimized and Nonoptimized Baseline Resource Allocations and Costs

Recruit Characteristics, Recruiting Mission and Resources	Nonoptimized Baseline Scenario	Optimized Baseline Scenario
USAR mission	15,000	15,000
RA mission	69,000	69,000
Percentage of HQ accessions target	67.9%	67.9%
Percentage of waivers	10%	10%
PS-CLG	800	800
Recruiters (average across fiscal year)	9,000	7,524
Recruiter costs (in millions of dollars)	1,002	838
Television prospect advertising costs (in millions of dollars)	131	128
Bonus costs (in millions of dollars)	44	41
Total costs (in millions of dollars)	1,177	1,006
Percentage of USAR accession goal achieved	107.8%	100%

NOTES: The nonoptimized baseline scenario allocations are determined using the baseline parameters set in the model by the user, assumed to remain constant through the fiscal year time horizon. Contract production of over 100 percent implies that the initial resource allocation set in the model is sufficient to meet mission objectives, but the objective function is not optimized. The optimized baseline scenario allocations are determined by the RRRM using the RRRM optimization algorithm. The model assumes that the number of initial recruiters is 9,000, and that initial television prospect advertising spending is $10.9 million in the month immediately preceding the start of the fiscal year, and the model uses the prevailing minimum wage in the baseline year.

- The distribution of recruiting spending changed to 83 percent, 13 percent, and 4 percent among recruiters ($838 million), television prospect advertising ($128 million), and MOS bonus incentives ($41 million). This implies that recruiters were overallocated in the baseline (9,000 per month on average relative to 7,524 at the optimum), while television prospect advertising spending was underallocated. Bonus spending levels, on a percentage basis, remained relatively unchanged.
- Costs per recruit drop from $72,800 to $67,000.

Results are mixed in terms of the time trends for each category of recruiting spending. Figure 5.1 shows the time trend for bonus amounts

FIGURE 5.1

Time Trends of Bonus Eligibility and Bonus Levels Within the Fiscal Year

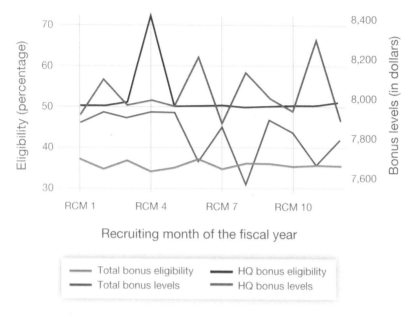

Recruiting month of the fiscal year

——— Total bonus eligibility   ——— HQ bonus eligibility
——— Total bonus levels   ——— HQ bonus levels

NOTE: Optimized baseline scenario results determined by the RRRM using the RRRM optimization algorithm.

and eligibility for all contracts and HQ contracts. For the most part, the algorithm keeps eligibility and bonus levels near the assumed baseline levels, but they "pulse" according to mission and the fixed effects associated with each month of the CPM in order to make mission. Average eligibility levels overall stay at 35 percent, but HQ eligibility averages 52 percent, largely due to the spike in recruiting contract month four.[9] This suggests that bonuses can be an effective short-run solution for USAR in order to

---

[9] Because mission and production are low during the winter holiday season, and the objective function penalizes deviations from monthly accession goals, the optimal solution is to spike bonus eligibility levels during this period to address production problems, which is not restricted in terms of month-to-month changes, as are recruiters, and which is more productive than advertising spending at this level of resourcing.

fill unit vacancies.[10] We further explore the use of bonuses in "incentive-centric" strategies to fill unit vacancies in later sections of this chapter.

Figure 5.2 shows the time trends for the other two recruiting resources. The number of recruiters monotonically decreases over the fiscal year, which can be explained by the facts that (1) monthly missions are generally greater in the first part of the fiscal year, and (2) changes in recruiter levels are "throttled" by the constraints on month-to-month changes to

FIGURE 5.2

Time Trends of Recruiters and Television Prospect Advertising Spending Within the Fiscal Year

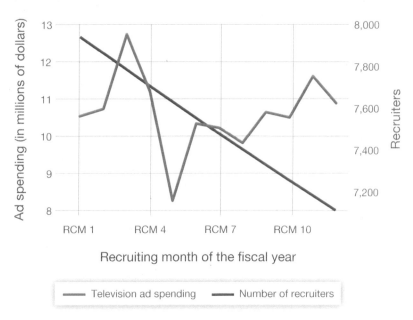

NOTE: Optimized baseline scenario results determined by the RRRM using the RRRM optimization algorithm.

---

[10] We note that given the structure of the model, there is no strategic behavior/anticipatory response on the part of recruits to changes in bonus utilization; rather, changes in the use of bonuses are determined by the marginal costs of generating contracts as implied by the CPM. In reality, to the extent that changes in bonus use were predictable, strategic behavior is likely. This is a potential area of research for future model iterations.

more realistically mimic workforce changes. As the optimization does not consider future fiscal years, which would begin with relatively high mission levels, this time trend in recruiters would likely not be optimal in real life, but it is illustrative that baseline recruiter levels are too high (i.e., resources are not optimized at baseline levels) for fulfilling only the USAR mission for a single fiscal year.[11]

Television prospect advertising faces no such constraints (though the advertising "stock" does depend on the previous month's spending levels) and varies over the fiscal year, from a low of just over $8.2 million in recruiting contract month five (February) to a high of $12.8 million in recruiting contract month three (December). The overall average of $10.6 million is lower than the initial allocation, again suggesting that the initial assumed monthly spending is too high to be efficient.

For the remainder of this chapter, unless otherwise noted, references to the baseline will denote the optimized baseline scenario results.

Alternative Accession Goals

In this section we explore the recruiting cost implications of increasing accession goals for both the USAR itself and the RA. Readers are reminded that the results apply only to USAR recruiting objectives.

Increasing U.S. Army Reserve Accession Goals

The first alternative accession goal excursion increases the total number of desired NPS contracts plus PS-CLG contracts from 15,000 to 25,000 (an increase reflecting prior production levels; see Table 2.1).

In this and all other excursions that increase the USAR mission, we assume that PS contracts increase proportionally with NPS contracts, such

---

[11] While we considered several workarounds, including a "carryover" penalty on the objective function and optimizing over multiple years, time and budget constraints prevented us from exploring this further. As recruiting resources are shared across the RA and USAR, however, the results here would likely not be used in the absence of information about how resource allocations affect the RA, and thus are largely illustrative of trade-offs in resource use for USAR. Future work will address this issue.

that they continue to constitute 5.33 percent of signed contracts. All other inputs are held at their baseline levels, and results are obtained using the optimization algorithm. Results for this excursion are presented in the first results column of Table 5.2, which holds RA mission at the 69,000 baseline.

Given such a large increase in mission, overall resource levels must increase by over $1 billion, from $1.006 billion to $2.144 billion, to meet USAR recruiting goals (an increase of 113 percent). Average cost per recruit

TABLE 5.2
Results from Alternative U.S. Army Reserve and Regular Army Accession Goals Excursions

Recruit Characteristics, Recruiting Mission, and Resources	Optimized High USAR Mission Scenario	Optimized High USAR and RA Mission Scenario	Optimized Baseline Scenario
USAR mission	25,000	25,000	15,000
RA mission	69,000	79,000	69,000
Percentage of HQ accessions target	67.9%	67.9%	67.9%
Percentage of waivers	10%	10%	10%
PS-CLG	1,333	1,333	800
Recruiters (average across fiscal year)	16,127	16,774	7,524
Recruiter costs (in millions of dollars)	1,795	1,867	838
Television prospect advertising costs (in millions of dollars)	238	229	128
Bonus costs (in millions of dollars)	111	110	41
Total costs (in millions of dollars)	2,144	2,206	1,006
Percentage of USAR accession goal achieved	100%	100%	100%

NOTES: The optimized scenario solutions are determined by the RRRM using the RRRM optimization algorithm. The model assumes that the number of initial recruiters is 9,000 and that initial television prospect advertising spending is $10.9 million in the month immediately preceding the start of the fiscal year, and the model uses the prevailing minimum wage in the baseline year.

increases to $85,800. This result is driven by the diminishing marginal returns of recruit resource spending—that is, as overall expenditures (and thus contracts) increase, the cost of the next contract increases. We do note, however, that while a 25,000 USAR mission for NPS and PS-CLG was more common in the early 2000s, before the Great Recession, these missioning goals were not seen during the FY 2012–FY 2018 period for which we have complete data. As such, this missioning is "out of sample" as far as predictions are concerned.

The final shares of recruiting resource spending shift slightly, with recruiters accounting for 84 percent of spending, television advertising accounting for 11 percent, and bonuses accounting for 5 percent. However, not all resource categories increased by the same percentage; recruiter spending was up by about the same percentage as total costs, but advertising spending increased by 86 percent and bonus spending by 171 percent. This can be explained by the relative slopes of the (implied) marginal cost curves of each resource at this level of spending, which are different from that of the baseline.

Increasing U.S. Army Reserve and Regular Army Accession Goals

The CPM results showed that as the RA mission increased, recruiters tended to shift attention toward those recruits at the expense of USAR contracts. The excursion presented in this section assumes that the RA increases its accession goal from 69,000 to 79,000 (a level near the 80,000-accession mission starting in FY 2018 and seen in FY 2005–FY 2008). We further assume that the USAR mission is increased to 25,000, as in the previous scenario. All other inputs are held at their baseline levels, and results are obtained using the optimization algorithm. Results are presented for this excursion in the second results column of Table 5.2.

A rise in RA mission of 10,000 would increase total recruiting costs by $62 million, holding constant the USAR mission at 25,000, and other variables are at baseline values. This involves reducing spending on bonuses and television advertising slightly, and increasing the number of recruiters, suggesting that the efficiency of using bonuses and television prospect advertising is very low at these levels of resource use and RA mission. In other words, the *relative* low elasticity and diminished marginal productivity of nonrecruiter resources as compared with that of recruiters when accession goals (and thus resource use) are high means that the cost-minimizing solution is to increase the number of recruiters. Average costs per recruit increase to $88,200. As such, should the Army be interested in achieving these recruiting goals, alternative strategies, such as loosening eligibility requirements, should be explored. We explore the effect of such a change in subsequent sections.

Television advertising and bonus expenditures decline because the change in RA mission increases their marginal cost relative to recruiters.[12] Functionally, the algorithm takes these changes into account in the optimization routine, reallocating among resources to obtain an optimized solution.

These results estimate the minimum resources needed (conditional on eligibility policy) to meet USAR missioning objectives. They do not account for also resourcing and meeting RA objectives, which use the same resources for recruiting. Providing this information on resource minimums can be instructive to planners contemplating the implications of changes in end strength for the costs of meeting the USAR accession requirement and the likely feasibility of meeting USAR missioning goals given a set of resources and RA accession objectives. Development of a joint recruiting model based on both the RA RRM and USAR RRM CPMs could provide information about a global optimum over both components.

Alternative Eligibility Policies

In this section we explore the cost implications to the Army of changing eligibility policy by increasing the waiver rate and decreasing the targeted percentage of HQ recruits. The USAR faces a trade-off when it comes to recruit quality, as increasing the percentage of HQ recruits (tightening eligibility policy) in theory requires more resources. The extent to which this is true, however, depends on the size of the accession goal and the difficulty of recruiting conditions. However, loosening eligibility requirements may be helpful in reducing the large cost increase associated with large increases in accession requirements as seen earlier. The proper interpretation of the

---

[12] Note that RA mission enters the CPM essentially as a factor of production rather than a contract production shifter that is resource neutral.

results that follow is to compare the results from alterative eligibility policies with the baseline results, with the increment indicating the change in minimum resource needs necessary to meet the USAR recruiting mission.

Increasing the Waiver Rate

The first eligibility policy change is to increase the waiver rate from a baseline of 10 percent to 20 percent.[13] In essence, assuming the baseline rate is binding, this increases the number of potential enlistees by making eligibility policy less restrictive and lowers the resource requirements necessary to reach accession goals. However, this may come with costs, such as separations involving medical or conduct issues, during the first term of service.

The first results column of Table 5.3 displays the results of this excursion. Recalling that baseline recruiting costs for a 15,000-accession mission are $1.006 billion, we see that expanding the use of waivers by 10 percentage points decreases overall recruiting costs by just over $200 million (about 20 percent). Because this policy effectively reduces overall resource needs to meet mission, the shares in each resource category change slightly, as the recruiter share decreases to 79 percent of total cost, television advertising spending increases to 16 percent of the total, and bonus costs increase to 5 percent of the total.

Decreasing the Target Percentage of High Quality Recruits

The second eligibility policy change is to decrease the percentage of HQ recruits from the baseline of 67.9 percent to 55.2 percent (the product of a five-point reduction in Tier 1 candidates to 92 percent, and 60 percent for I–IIIAs, the Office of the Secretary of Defense–established floor for I–IIIAs). This change is an alternative way to loosen eligibility requirements for accessions, which comes with an attrition and capability cost, as education tier is highly correlated with attrition and AFQT score is highly correlated with job performance (Orvis et al., 2018).

---

[13] Although we do not distinguish between medical and conduct waivers in the CPM, medical waivers accounted for between 80 and 85 percent of all waivers during the FY 2013–FY 2018 period. Nonfelony conduct waivers constitute a large majority of remaining waivers granted during this period.

The middle column of Table 5.3 displays the results for this excursion. As is true for increasing the waiver percentage, this policy reduces minimum costs, in this case by about $129 million. As such, it pushes the relative shares of total costs across categories toward the baseline relative to the waiver policy.

TABLE 5.3

Results from Excursions That Lower Eligibility Requirements

Recruit Characteristics, Recruiting Mission, and Resources	Waivers Increase to 20%	HQ Accession Goal Decreases to 55.2%	Both Eligibility Policies Change	Optimized Baseline Scenario
USAR mission	15,000	15,000	15,000	15,000
RA mission	69,000	69,000	69,000	69,000
Percentage of HQ accessions target	67.9%	55.2%	55.2%	67.9%
Percentage of waivers	20%	10%	20%	10%
PS-CLG	800	800	800	800
Recruiters (average across fiscal year)	5,688	6,385	4,912	7,524
Recruiter costs (in millions of dollars)	633	710	547	838
Television prospect advertising costs (in millions of dollars)	127	125	114	128
Bonus costs (in millions of dollars)	40	41	39	41
Total costs (in millions of dollars)	799	877	700	1,006
Percentage of USAR accession goal achieved	100%	100%	100%	100%

NOTES: The optimized scenario solutions are determined by the RRRM using the RRRM optimization algorithm. The model assumes that the number of initial recruiters is 9,000 and that initial television prospect advertising spending is $10.9 million in the month immediately preceding the start of the fiscal year, and the model uses the prevailing minimum wage in the baseline year.

Increasing Eligibility Using Waivers and Share of High Quality Recruits

The final excursion in the eligibility section imposes both the waiver policy and the HQ recruit share policy at the same time. As seen in Table 5.3, the overall financial costs necessary to meet the accession goals decline by about $306 million, or just over 30 percent of baseline recruiting costs. Recruiter shares of total costs fall to 78 percent, television advertising rises to 16 percent of the total, and bonus use increases to 6 percent of recruiting spending. This equates to an average recruiting cost of $46,700, a decrease of $20,400 (30 percent) over the optimized baseline.

The optimized results for USAR do not address the sufficiency of the resources to support the RA mission at current mission and eligibility policy. As such, this scenario simply illustrates that restricting eligibility through medical and conduct exclusions and maintaining a high target share of USAR HQ recruits is financially costly from a recruiting standpoint. The optimality of such policies also depends on the opportunity costs in terms of attrition, capability, and waiver-related early separations.[14] Given the results on potential cost savings of changes in eligibility policies, we next explore what happens to recruiting costs when eligibility policies are relaxed and accession goals for USAR and the RA are high.

Using Eligibility Policy to Meet High Accession Goals at Lower Financial Costs

This excursion investigates the cost implications of using eligibility policy to lower the minimum costs of meeting USAR accession objectives when both RA and USAR accession levels are high (79,000 for the RA, 25,000 for USAR). Recall from earlier sections that the optimized average recruit cost for USAR when missioning was expanded was $87,760, or a total of $2.194 billion. Increasing eligibility through policies such as increasing the waiver rate or decreasing the share of HQ recruits should, as seen in Table 5.3 for baseline conditions, decrease total minimum resource levels

---

[14] These implications are analyzed in unpublished RAND Corporation research.

necessary to meet USAR accession objectives (while also potentially increasing other costs associated with lowering the quality of accessions based on the changes in eligibility).

Table 5.4 documents two examples. In the first results column, we reproduce the scenario with expanded mission and low eligibility reported in Table 5.2. In the second results column, we show the impact of increasing

TABLE 5.4

Results from Alternative U.S. Army Reserve and Regular Army Accession Goals and Eligibility Excursions

Recruit Characteristics, Recruiting Mission, and Resources	Optimized High USAR and RA Mission Scenario, Low Eligibility	Optimized High USAR and RA Mission Scenario, High Eligibility	Optimized Baseline Scenario
USAR mission	25,000	25,000	15,000
RA mission	79,000	79,000	69,000
Percentage of HQ accessions target	67.9%	55.2%	67.9%
Percentage of waivers	10%	20%	10%
PS-CLG	1,333	1,333	800
Recruiters (average across fiscal year)	16,774	10,171	7,524
Recruiter costs (in millions of dollars)	1,867	1,132	838
Television prospect advertising costs (in millions of dollars)	229	193	128
Bonus costs (in millions of dollars)	110	60	41
Total costs (in millions of dollars)	2,206	1,386	1,006
Percentage of USAR accession goal achieved	100%	100%	100%

NOTES: The optimized scenario solutions are determined by the RRRM using the RRRM optimization algorithm. The model assumes that the number of initial recruiters is 9,000 and that initial television prospect advertising spending is $10.9 million in the month immediately preceding the start of the fiscal year, and the model uses the prevailing minimum wage in the baseline year.

eligibility by increasing the waiver rate to 20 percent and decreasing the share of HQ recruits to 55.2 percent (as in the previous section).

The results are fairly dramatic. Overall minimum resource levels drop by just over $800 million (37 percent) when compared with a low-eligibility scenario, with overall minimum resource levels calculated at about $380 million more than baseline mission. In other words, the 10,000 additional recruits cost an average of $38,000 each (relative to the costs associated with baseline mission and eligibility). Overall, under this new missioning and eligibility scenario, average recruit costs decrease to $55,400, although the quality distribution is different.[15] Of the savings from the low-eligibility scenario, 79 percent come from the reduction in recruiters, from 15,719 to 10,171. The final distribution of spending is 82 percent recruiters (10,171 recruiters on average), 14 percent television advertising spending, and 4 percent bonuses. It thus appears that a large expansion of both the RA and USAR missions may well necessitate a change in eligibility requirements so long as budgets are constrained. Again, we remind the reader that the cost changes shown in Table 5.4 do not account for costs associated with changes in attrition related to the recruit eligibility changes or for changes in behavioral outcomes over the enlistment term. The USAR costs were analyzed in unpublished RAND corporation research.

Alternative Resourcing Strategies

Knapp et al. (2018) investigated the implications of the Army's historical incentive-centric policy in which, primarily, bonuses are manipulated to reach problematic accession goals. We repeat a similar exercise for USAR. In the prior report, recruiters were kept at their initial levels, television advertising prospect spending was set to zero, and the (RA) model only manipulated bonus spending (within the allowable limits) to reach accession goals. In the second stage, the model optimized over the other two resource categories, but total bonus spending was restricted to be at least as high as in the first stage.

---

[15] In other words, relative to the optimized baseline USAR mission scenario with a mission of 15,000, the eligibility change lowers the marginal costs (of the 10,000 extra accessions in the high-mission, high-eligibility scenario) of adding contracts, pulling down both the costs of the 10,000 increment and the overall costs of accessing 25,000 recruits.

These results can be compared with the fully optimized results to illustrate the potential opportunity costs of "overuse" of incentives, either unintendedly or because the other nonbonus resources cannot be changed quickly enough to ensure that accession goals are met or because they are not in funds directly under the Army's control.

In running these excursions for USAR, we model the use of bonus incentives by keeping the "public goods"–inputs into contract production used by both USAR and RA–fixed and optimize over bonus levels. As such, we fix the number of recruiters at the baseline of 9,000 and advertising spending at $10.9 million per month and investigate the impact of using bonus incentives on total minimum resource requirements to fill any remaining gaps between accessions and contracts.

We explore two excursions in this section. The first assumes baseline parameters, while the second uses high accession targets for both USAR and RA, coupled with low eligibility. We compare each with the appropriate optimized scenarios to illustrate the differential in resource use to meet accession goals.

The Incentive-Centric Baseline

The first incentive-centric policy assessment explores the opportunity costs associated with bonus use using the baseline parameterization (Table 5.5). When recruiters are restricted to be fixed at 9,000, television prospect advertising spending is fixed at $131 million per year, and bonuses are maximized, the optimal solution found by the algorithm is 15,660 contracts at a resource cost of $1.170 billion, or approximately 16 percent over the optimized minimum resource requirements. This solution is above missioning objectives as a result of setting recruiters and television advertising spending above their optimal levels, coupled with the weights used in the objective function (especially those that are used to penalize monthly accession shortfalls as opposed to overall mission shortfalls). In reality, USAR might decide not to sign the extra contracts, and to the extent those contracts are associated with bonus spending, minimum resource costs for meeting the mission may be slightly lower.

While overall resource levels are higher given the fixed nature of recruiters and advertising spending, we note that overall bonus spending relative to the fully optimized scenario is lower. This is a result of the optimization

TABLE 5.5

Results from Baseline Mission Incentive-Centric Excursions

Recruit Characteristics, Recruiting Mission and Resources	Optimized Baseline Scenario	Optimized Incentive-Centric Baseline Scenario
USAR Mission	15,000	15,000
RA Mission	69,000	69,000
Percentage of HQ accessions target	67.9%	67.9%
Percentage of waivers	10%	10%
PS-CLG	800	800
Recruiters (average across fiscal year)	7,524	9,000
Recruiter costs (in millions of dollars)	838	1,002
Television prospect advertising costs (in millions of dollars)	128	131
Bonus costs (in millions of dollars)	41	37
Total costs (in millions of dollars)	1,006	1,170
Percentage of USAR accession goal achieved	100%	104%

NOTES: The optimized scenario solutions are determined by the RRRM using the RRRM optimization algorithm over the dimensions indicated in the column titles. The optimized baseline incentive-centric scenario fixed recruiters and television advertising spending at baseline levels and optimizes over the use of bonuses. The model assumes that the number of initial recruiters is 9,000 and that initial television prospect advertising spending is $10.9 million in the month immediately preceding the start of the fiscal year, and the model uses the prevailing minimum wage in the baseline year.

routine attempting to decrease excess contracts (subject to the objective function) and the associated costs through reduction of bonus levels. This is expected given that the number of contracts produced from the nonoptimized baseline scenario is also greater than the target level.

The Incentive-Centric High Accession Target with Low Eligibility

The second incentive-centric policy explores the opportunity costs associated with bonus use using a parameterization that includes high accession targets (79,000 for the RA and 25,000 for USAR) coupled with the relatively low eligibility baseline of nearly 68 percent HQ and 10 percent waivers. We follow the procedures of the previous section in reporting these results and compare this excursion with the optimized results for higher accession objectives reported in Table 5.2. In the event that the optimized incentive-centric scenario does not meet the overall mission, we set bonus eligibility and levels as high as possible. Results are reported in Table 5.6.

TABLE 5.6

Results from High Regular Army and U.S. Army Reserve Mission Incentive-Centric Excursions

Recruit Characteristics, Recruiting Mission and Resources	Optimized High USAR and RA Mission Scenario	Optimized Incentive-Centric High Mission Scenario	Maximum Bonus Scenario	Optimized Baseline Scenario
USAR mission	25,000	25,000	25,000	15,000
RA mission	79,000	79,000	79,000	69,000
Percentage of HQ accessions target	67.9%	67.9%	67.9%	67.9%
Percentage of waivers	10%	10%	10%	10%
PS-CLG	1,333	1,333	1,333	800
Recruiters (average across fiscal year)	15,719	9,000	9,000	7,524
Recruiter costs (in millions of dollars)	1,750	1,002	1,002	838
Television prospect advertising costs (in millions of dollars)	200	131	131	128
Bonus costs (in millions of dollars)	219	150	310	41
Total costs (in millions of dollars)	2,168	1,283	1,443	1,006
Percentage of USAR accession goal achieved	100%	77%	77%	100%

NOTES: The optimized scenario solutions are determined by the RRRM using the RRRM optimization algorithm over the dimensions indicated in the column titles. The optimized high-mission incentive-centric scenario fixes recruiters and television advertising spending at baseline levels and optimizes over the use of bonuses. The maximum bonus scenario sets bonus eligibility and levels at their maximum. The model assumes that the number of initial recruiters is 9,000 and that initial television prospect advertising spending is $10.9 million in the month immediately preceding the start of the fiscal year, and the model uses the prevailing minimum wage in the baseline year.

The fully optimized high-mission solution presented earlier (in the first results column) satisfied both total and HQ missioning objectives at a total minimum resource requirement of $2.168 billion using greater-than-baseline numbers of recruiters and television prospect advertising spending. This is the minimum cost of meeting the 25,000 and 79,000 accession goals when all resource levels are optimized. At the assumed incentive-centric resourcing and bonus levels, and assuming that maximum bonuses are paid (costing $400 million in bonus dollars), total resource costs would be $1.533. However, the accession mission is not met because this figure is lower than the minimum cost of achieving mission. We therefore conclude that meeting these high levels of missioning are not feasible for USAR under the assumptions of the incentive-centric scenarios, which mimic recent conditions.

More specifically, we present two examples of trade-offs in light of this infeasibility. The first, labeled "Optimized Incentive-Centric High Mission Scenario" in Table 5.6, relies on the optimization algorithm to determine, subject to the weights on the objective function, the affordable number of accessions. In this solution, only 77 percent of the overall and HQ accession missions is achieved at a resource requirement of just over $1.2 billion. We note that bonuses are not maximized in this solution, as the marginal costs of using them relative to the implied willingness to pay in the objective function is too high.[16] As a result, only 19,330 USAR contracts are produced.

The option in the third column, labeled "Maximum Bonus Scenario," sets bonus eligibility and bonus levels to their constrained maximums. In this solution, slightly more contracts are produced than in the optimized incentive-centric scenario (19,362, versus 19,330 overall), but mission is still not feasible according to the CPM. Total resource requirements increase to just over $1.4 billion. We note that because fewer than 25,000 contracts are produced, total spending on bonuses is not at the (theoretical) maximum level for 25,000 accessions.

Overall, these results show that while bonus spending can induce USAR contract production, using only bonus spending without considering the marginal costs associated with other means of doing so (namely, changing the

---

[16] An equivalent statement is that the marginal productivity of using bonuses to generate contracts at these resource levels are quite low, and it is better (in terms of the objective function) to fall short of mission targets rather than incur these costs.

number of recruiters, using television advertising, and considering accession eligibility policy changes) is likely an inefficient means of reaching accession goals. However, bonuses can (and should) be used in a strategic manner to reach monthly and overall USAR accession goals, especially as these incentives are at the individual contract level and under the Army's direct control. Based on results presented here, the share of bonus spending for cost-minimizing resource requirements for USAR is likely in the range of 4–6 percent depending on the mission objectives and eligibility policies in play for conditions similar to what is modeled herein.[17] However, when other resources are fixed from the USAR's perspective (for example, due to RA recruiting requirements), an efficient solution for USAR may not be possible. In that case, the optimal bonus share for USAR may be higher or lower than the values obtained, or USAR accession goals may not be attainable.

Chapter Summary

The RRRM produces monthly USAR accessions for a specified level of recruiting resources, enlistment eligibility policies, the RA mission, variables related to the recruiting environment, and the USAR unit vacancy fill distribution over time. When optimized, the RRRM can be used by Army planners to compare the minimum resourcing needs and the feasibility of meeting USAR mission objectives across a range of assumptions about these variables.

This chapter has illustrated some of the possibilities of how the RRRM can be used for considering trade-offs among the levels and mix of recruiting resources and between resource use and recruit eligibility policy decisions when filling USAR unit vacancies. Among our major findings are the following:

- The minimum resource requirement necessary to meet baseline USAR accession objectives based on recent data and a relatively strict eligibility policy is just over $1 billion, distributed among recruiters (83 percent), television advertising prospect spending (13 percent), and bonuses (4 percent).

---

[17] Note that this does not take into account the resources needed by the RA to meet its accession objectives.

- Increasing the recruiting mission significantly increases USAR recruiting resource requirements, but optimizing over the resource mix shows that minimum resource requirements for USAR do not scale up proportionally. Furthermore, changes in RA mission affect the minimum requirements per USAR recruit, with a 10,000 RA accession increment increasing USAR recruiting resource requirements by about 2.9 percent when the USAR mission is 25,000.
- Current eligibility policy for the USAR is relatively strict; increasing the waiver rate to 20 percent (from 10 percent) and lowering the HQ percentage from 67.9 percent to 55.2 percent can decrease recruiting costs by about 30 percent. However, this figure does not include any potential attrition and performance costs associated with lower-quality recruits.
- Eligibility policy can be used to significantly decrease minimum resource requirements in times of large missions, with cost savings for our example of about 37 percent.
- When recruiting resource inputs are shared by the RA and USAR and are thus fixed from the perspective of USAR, MOS bonuses can be used by USAR to try to reach its accession goals. However, depending on the size of both the RA and USAR missions, costs per recruit may be considerably higher than minimum requirements, or mission shortfalls may result.[18]

There are several caveats and limitations to highlight about the RRRM. First, the analysis in this report only optimizes recruiting resources to satisfy USAR recruiting mission requirements (albeit conditional on RA mission). Given that the number of recruiters and television advertising spending affect both components' contract production, it is unlikely that the optimized results presented herein are either qualitatively or quantitatively consistent with minimizing costs across the joint mission. Future work could include integration of the RA RRM and RRRM by defining a joint objective function, with the CPMs from each component incorporated into the joint model.

---

[18] Unless otherwise noted in the summary results, baseline parameters are held constant.

Second, the RRRM is based on past data, and the CPM gives average company-level responses to changes in the recruiting environment, resources, and eligibility policy. There is no guarantee that past relationships will remain constant in the future or that there will be no local or other constraints that may manifest in the future and affect contract production. The geographical distribution of recruiting companies, recruiters, advertising viewership, population, and missioning rates, as well as recruiter costs, could change in the future, which may make the CPM and RRRM less representative of any future reality. The relationship of especially younger recruits to advertising messaging as digital forms of advertising evolve, and the means by which content is consumed has already changed notably from FY 2012 to FY 2018 (the period of our data). In addition, the model assumes that eligibility policy constrains supply; the extent to which this is true in reality likely depends on the waiver rate or recruit quality targets. However, we note that even the higher eligibility rates we use are still well above the national average for U.S. youth. We use a high school graduation rate for recruits of 92 percent and an AFQT I–IIIA (upper-fifty percentiles) rate of 60 percent for recruits, whereas the rates among U.S. youth are 85 percent and 50 percent, respectively.

Third, we note that while only the local minimum wage was significant as a recruiting environment variable in the current study, this may not be the case as more (and different) data become available. The FY 2012–FY 2018 period was characterized by decreasing unemployment nationally, and that may obscure some true (but inestimable) relationships. Future research should continue to test for responses to these primarily economic variables.

Fourth, solutions to the model are conditional on the weights and subobjectives included in the objective function. The current parameterization prioritizes meeting yearly accession objectives, with smaller but significant penalties for not meeting monthly goals. This allows for contract substitution between recruiting months, but the relative values of the weighting parameters determine the exact recruiting resource mix. We encourage users of the RRRM to engage in sensitivity analysis when using the model for planning purposes.

Finally, as with all models, users should be wary of false precision. While the RRRM is based on real-world data and has been tested for reasonableness, model results are best used to illustrate trade-offs between strategic decisions and not to predict specific outcomes with analytic precision.

The RRRM is a structural mathematical costing model with relationships estimated by past data on the recruiting environment, resource use, policy, and USAR contracting. Mirroring a similar model for the RA (in Knapp et al., 2018), the RRRM tool can provide valuable information to Army planners about the trade-offs associated with the level and distribution of minimum recruiting resources and related policy decisions used to meet the USAR recruiting mission. Although the model does not yet optimize over the RA and USAR jointly, the RRRM can still be used to assess the impact of changes in resourcing and policy on the minimum level and distribution of resources needed to meet USAR NPS and PS-CLG accession goals. This information can be used to evaluate whether current or planned resourcing levels are sufficient to meet USAR recruiting goals, and how changes in resource levels and distributions, as well as eligibility policies, are likely to affect USAR accessions.

CHAPTER SIX

Conclusions and Recommendations

The Army's recruiting enterprise is the largest among the military services. Over the past five years, the USAR has had a USAREC enlisted recruiting mission averaging 15,200 enlisted soldiers each year. It is worth noting that recent recruiting requirements have been much lower than in the past—for example, in the period ten years earlier, from FY 2006 to FY 2010, when the annual USAREC USAR recruiting mission averaged 23,300 soldiers. While recent accession requirements have been lower, the demand for quality recruits has risen and the recruiting market has changed. The unemployment rate fell to below 4 percent, which stresses recruiting for the RA, which in turn stresses recruiting for USAR. At the same time, planned enlistment waiver rates have remained low, which, if binding, puts further pressure on the number of potential recruits.

The resources used to attract new enlistees, such as recruiters, bonuses, and advertising, differ both in their productivity and in the time required between the decision to use a resource and the ability to do so, as well as between resource use and enlistment response.[1] As discussed in the RA RRM report (Knapp et al., 2018), the Army spent on average $1.6 billion annually in 2020 dollars on recruiting resources (including recruiter compensation) from FY 2001 to FY 2014, and nearly $2.0 billion annually in FY 2008 and

---

[1] Advertising must be purchased, aired, and seen by enough youth for enough time to have an effect, and some of that effect is lagged over the next several months. Recruiters in place have fixed tour lengths, and new recruiters must be identified, trained, moved to the location of their recruiting assignment, and recruit for several months before they become effective.

FY 2009.[2] In the past, the Army has limited recruit eligibility in good recruiting environments to increase recruit quality. In contrast, during difficult recruiting times the Army has increased eligibility to help ensure achievement of the accession requirement. This has included additional enlistment waivers, more enlistments among persons with prior military service, and more Tier 2 recruits and recruits scoring below the fiftieth percentile on the AFQT.

Understanding how recruiting resources and enlistment eligibility policies work in concert and how the optimal levels and mix of recruiting resources vary under different recruiting requirements, eligibility policies, and environments is key in enabling decisionmakers to use the Army's limited resources to effectively and efficiently achieve the Army's accession requirements. The RRRM discussed in this report considers the relationships among the monthly level and mix of recruiting resources, recruiting environment, recruit eligibility policies, accumulated contracts, and unit vacancy fill targets and models the joint influence of these factors on monthly accessions realized.

The RRRM consists of contract production and cost allocation submodels. The contract production submodel considers trade-offs between recruiting conditions and the resources needed to produce total and HQ enlistment contracts under given recruit eligibility policies. The cost allocation submodel accounts for the resourcing costs incurred in order to achieve the fiscal year's enlistment contracts and accessions.

The RRRM alone only predicts whether a resourcing plan is adequate to achieve an accession mission. Determining efficient allocations of resources also requires an optimization algorithm. This algorithm is designed to find the cost-minimizing levels and mix of recruiting resources conditional on the recruiting environment and the Army's recruit eligibility policies. The algorithm has two objectives: (1) to produce enough accessions to fill each month's unit vacancies, and (2) to minimize total costs. The combination of the RRRM and the optimization algorithm make up the RRRM tool.

We demonstrate how the RRRM can be used to analyze success in meeting an accession goal for a specified resourcing plan. We also provide three

---

[2]   As noted earlier, recruiters, advertising, and enlistment bonuses offered to prospective recruits peaked in FY 2007–FY 2008. Because bonuses of $10,000 to $20,000 are paid over time, the actual costs incurred by the Army will be somewhat lower than the commitment cost at contract signing due to attrition.

examples illustrating how the RRRM tool can be used to assess potential resource and policy trade-offs. The examples include cost trade-offs based on

1. alternative accession goals
2. alternative recruit eligibility policies
3. alternative resourcing strategies.

These examples demonstrate the versatility of the RRRM tool in considering trade-offs. The RRRM can provide resourcing alternatives that can meet accession goals while potentially saving hundreds of millions of dollars. The RRRM together with the RA RRM therefore are valuable additions to the Army's planning tools, though future research should link the two, since the RA and USAR share recruiting resources.

This report discusses examples that illustrate important strategic-level trade-offs. As the difficulty level of recruiting changes in response to accession requirement changes, effectiveness and efficiency require different levels and mixes of recruiting resources and enlistment eligibility policies. Army planners can use the RRRM tool to consider the potential cost and resourcing requirements of a variety of recruiting contingencies. Our example of alternative resourcing strategies shows how a strategy emphasizing one resource over others (e.g., reliance on bonuses because of their shorter lead time when policymakers react to difficult recruiting conditions rather than planning for them in advance) can be much more costly than using a mix of resources. We also illustrate how changing recruit eligibility policies can substantially reduce recruiting resource costs. The RRRM, when used in combination with the Reserve Recruit Selection Tooles (described in unpublished RAND Corporation research), enables policymakers to consider changes in first-term costs and performance associated with broadening recruit eligibility, as well as related changes in recruiting costs.

The RRRM provides help to Army leaders in shaping a cost-efficient strategy that can achieve USAR accession requirements. Continued success of the RRRM tool will require updating the model to reflect the current effectiveness of recruiting resources. Future refinements could also include integration with existing planning and budgeting models. This would enable the RRRM tool's use as a budgeting resource in addition to a strategic resource.

References

Arkes, Jeremy and M. Rebecca Kilburn, *Modeling Reserve Recruiting: Estimates of Enlistments*, Santa Monica, Calif.: RAND Corporation, MG-202-OSD, 2005. As of March 10, 2022:
https://www.rand.org/pubs/monographs/MG202.html

Asch, Beth J., Paul Heaton, James Hosek, Paco Martorell, Curtis Simon, and John T. Warner, *Cash Incentives and Military Enlistment, Attrition, and Reenlistment*, Santa Monica, Calif.: RAND Corporation, MG-950-OSD, 2010. As of February 2, 2022:
https://www.rand.org/pubs/monographs/MG950.html

Asch, Beth J., James R. Hosek, and John T. Warner, "New Economics of Manpower in the Post-Cold War Era," in Todd Sandler and Keith Harley, eds., *Handbook of Defense Economics*, Amsterdam: Elsevier, 2007, pp. 1076–1138.

Curtin, Richard, "Consumer Sentiment Surveys: Worldwide Review and Assessment," *Journal of Business Cycle Measurement and Analysis*, Vol. 3, No. 1, 2007, pp. 7–24.

Dertouzos, James N., *The Cost-Effectiveness of Military Advertising: Evidence from 2002–2004*, Santa Monica, Calif.: RAND Corporation, DB-565-OSD, 2009. As of February 2, 2022:
https://www.rand.org/pubs/documented_briefings/DB565.html

Dertouzos, James N., and Steven Garber, *Is Military Advertising Effective? An Estimation Methodology and Applications to Recruiting in the 1980s and 90s*, Santa Monica, Calif.: RAND Corporation, MR-1591-OSD, 2003. As of February 2, 2022:
https://www.rand.org/pubs/monograph_reports/MR1591.html

DoDI—*See* Department of Defense Instruction.

Gilroy, Curtis, Elizabeth Clelan, Josh Horvath, and Christopher Gonzales, *The All-Volunteer Force and the Need for Sustained Investment in Recruiting*, Arlington, Va.: Center for Naval Analyses, 2020.

Joint Advertising Market Research & Studies, *The Target Population for Military Recruitment: Youth Eligible to Enlist Without a Waiver*, Seaside, Calif.: Defense Manpower Data Center, 2016.

Knapp, David, Bruce R. Orvis, Christopher E. Maerzluft, and Tiffany Tsai, *Resources Required to Meet the U.S. Army's Enlisted Recruiting Requirements Under Alternative Recruiting Goals, Conditions, and Eligibility Policies*, Santa Monica, Calif.: RAND Corporation, RR-2364-A, 2018. As of October 2, 2018:
https://www.rand.org/pubs/research_reports/RR2364.html

Neumark, David, "Datasets and Code Teaching," web database, University of California–Irvine, undated. As of March 15, 2021:
http://www.economics.uci.edu/~dneumark/datasets.html

Orvis, Bruce R., Christopher Maerzluft, Sung-Bou Kim, Michael G. Shanley, and Heather Krull, *Prospective Outcome Assessment for Alternative Recruit Selection Policies*, Santa Monica, Calif.: RAND Corporation, RR-2267-A, 2018. As of October 2, 2018:
https://www.rand.org/pubs/research_reports/RR2267.html

Polich, J. Michael, James N. Dertouzos, and S. James Press, *The Enlistment Bonus Experiment*, Santa Monica, Calif.: RAND Corporation, R-3353-FMP, 1986. As of February 2, 2022:
https://www.rand.org/pubs/reports/R3353.html

Powell, M. J. D., "A Direct Search Optimization Method That Models the Objective and Constraint Functions by Linear Interpolation," in Susana Gomez and Jean-Pierre Hennart, eds., *Mathematics and Its Applications*: Vol. 275, *Advances in Optimization and Numerical Analysis*. Dordrecht, Netherlands: Springer, 1994, pp. 51–67.

Shapiro, B., G.J. Hitsch, and A. Tuchman, "Generalizable and Robust TV Advertising Effects." NBER Working Paper 27684, Cambridge, Mass: National Bureau of Economic Research, 2020.

U.S. Department of Defense, "Military Compensation: Greenbooks," web database, undated. As of February 13, 2022:
https://militarypay.defense.gov/References/Greenbooks/

Warner, John, Curtis Simon, and Deborah Payne, *Enlistment Supply in the 1990's: A Study of the Navy College Fund and Other Enlistment Incentive Programs*, Arligton, Va.: Defense Manpower Data Center, DMDC Report No. 2000-015, 2001.

———, "The Military Recruiting Productivity Slowdown: The Roles of Resources, Opportunity Cost, and the Tastes of Youth*," *Defence and Peace Economics*, Vol. 14, No. 5, 2003, pp. 329–342.

Wenger, Jeffrey B., David Knapp, Parag Mahajan, Bruce R. Orvis, and Tiffany Berglund, "Developing a National Recruiting Difficulty Index," Santa Monica, Calif.: RAND Corporation, RR-2637-A, 2019. As of March 30, 2022:
https://www.rand.org/pubs/research_reports/RR2637.html